Retreat Leader Guide
WORKBOOK

RICHARD T. CASE

Dedication/Acknowledgments

As an expression of my gratitude, I wish to dedicate this course to my wife, Linda, and our ministry leaders who are living in the Kingdom of God. We all live in the kingdom of the world, under the sway, control, and authority of the enemy. As believers we are called to live in the Kingdom of God—a spiritual kingdom that is preeminent and superior to the kingdom of the world. In the gospels, Jesus spoke often of the kingdom (more so than most any other thing). We are to live in both places (which is why we cannot be removed from this world and the trouble/difficulties of this world). Rather than just live in the natural and always struggle through life in the kingdom of the world, we are to live in the spiritual kingdom of God that provides the superior power to resolve all struggles and have us enjoy all aspects of our lives. In order to be in the kingdom, we must surrender our will, and then follow the King of the Kingdom (and thus it is not us). When we are living in the kingdom of God, we have remarkable privileges and benefits that provide hope, excitement, and great adventure. Linda and the ministry team demonstrate this life of the kingdom (because they live in His kingdom) and then teach others this critical truth. Once understood, it makes all the difference in life. Their faithfulness continually reminds us all of the beauty of this life available to us as we walk in the kingdom. Thank you, Linda and the ministry team for helping us all understand the difference between just living in the kingdom of the world that is trouble, and living in the Kingdom, which is righteousness, peace, and joy in the Holy Spirit.

These leaders are:
Jake and Mary Beckel
Joe and Leigh Bogar
Heath and Rebecca Cardie
Rich and Janet Cocchiaro
Larry and Sherry Collett
Scott and Kristen Cornell
David and Melissa Dunkel
Tom and Susanne Ewing
Rick and Kelly Ferris
Joel and Christina Gunn
Scott and Terry Hitchcock
Rick and Nancy Hoover
Tad and Monica Jones
Ed and Becky Kobel
Don and Rachelle Light
Chris and Heidi May
Terry and Josephine Noetzel
Towanda Norton
Steve and Carolyn Van Ooteghem
Preston and Lynda Pitts
Dan and Kathy Rocconi
Bob and Keri Rockwell
John and Michelle Santaferraro
Allyson and Denny Weinberg
Neal and Kathy Weisenburger

LIVING IN THE KINGDOM: Righteousness, Peace, and Joy in the Holy Spirit
PUBLISHED BY LIVING WATERS—ABIDE MINISTRIES
7615 Lemon Gulch Way
Castle Rock, CO 80108

ISBN: 979-8-218-12886-9

Printed in the United States of America 2024 — 2nd ed

TABLE OF CONTENTS

Welcome to our course, Living in the Kingdom of God—Righteousness, Peace, and Joy, which actually is stated in Romans 14:17—the Kingdom of God is righteousness, peace, and joy in the Holy Spirit. We're going to discuss exactly what this Kingdom is, how it relates to the kingdom of the world, the benefits of God's Kingdom, what it looks like, what God wants to deliver to us in that Kingdom, how we are supposed to live in that Kingdom, and the consequences of not doing so.

Let's start with defining righteousness. How would you define righteousness? Peace? Joy?

____

____

____

____

____

____

____

____

____

____

Righteousness:

Through God's righteousness (holiness), we can have a relationship with Him, a Covenant relationship where He blesses us to make us a blessing for others. He's going to deliver to us His life of righteousness so that we can live in the Covenant. As we read throughout the Old Testament, we are to seek and receive God and His righteousness, which is born out of His Covenant relationship with us.

> "Those who received His righteousness received it because of the sacrifices they made."

If you'd like to know more about
Abide Ministries,
please see our pages
at the back of the workbook

Those who received His righteousness received it because of the sacrifices they made. Ultimately, as David expressed, sacrifice was really a heart issue—surrendering to His will. The New Testament goes even deeper. Who is righteous? He is. In order for us to experience righteousness, we must have what? We must have Him. We must be clothed with Him. We must be walking with Him and His righteousness—born out of that Covenant relationship. In Romans 3:23 and 6:23, it states that no one is righteous. No, not one. So, can you earn it? Can you perform to it? No, in both the Old and New Testaments, God is delivering righteousness. If we look at the Hebrew and Greek words they have slightly different meanings. *Sadik* is wholeness, holiness. As we remain on that Covenant path as determined by God, *sadik* is deliverance, victory, prosperity, redemption from God through His Covenant with us. Those are the two words that are used in the Old Testament. The Greek is the condition acceptable to God, which is His life, His righteousness. Receiving this so that we can live in relationship with Him, in His Covenant.

Peace:

The word *peace* in the Old Testament is *shalom*. In the New Testament it is *eiriene*. They mean the same thing. The word *shalom* is: He's going to give us the Covenant life. He's going to bless us to make us a blessing. There's going to be wholeness. There's going to be completeness. There'll be prosperity in the sense of freedom. There'll be health and contentment. Our relationships will be in harmony. We can stay in shalom because it's different coming from God than it is coming from the world. God's shalom brings complete resolution to every situation, including conflict and opposing relationships—peace and favor from Him.

Joy:

The word *joy* means rejoicing, having excitement, exultation, enjoying life at an emotional level —enjoying this life of God. Does this depend on our circumstances? No. Because He says there's a different way for Him to help us understand and live out joy in spite of our circumstances. Worldly joy can be stolen because the focus is on the world, which brings trouble and unpleasantness that diminish His joy. Despite living in the world where we will have trouble, we can still have joy. The Old Testament word is *rejoice*. Be glad, have joy, mirth, and gaiety. In a sense, we're having a big party. In the New Testament, the word *cara* means joy, occasions of joy, gladness, well-being, thriving through the work of the Spirit.

How do the following verses describe:

> **1. Who is the Christ who is coming into the world?**
>
> **2. How did the heavenly hosts respond to Him coming?**
>
> **3. What was Christ bringing to the people of the world?**
>
> **4. What is the significance of this as we begin to understand the Kingdom of God?**

Read Luke 2:8–14:

The Shepherds and the Angels

8 And in the same region there were shepherds out in the field, keeping watch over their flock by night. 9 And an angel of the Lord appeared to them, and the glory of the Lord shone around them, and they were filled with great fear. 10 And the angel said to them, "Fear not, for behold, I bring you good news of great joy that will be for all the people. 11 For unto you is born this day in the city of David a Savior, who is Christ the Lord. 12 And this will be a sign for you: you will find a baby wrapped in swaddling cloths and lying in a manger." 13 And suddenly there was with the angel a multitude of the heavenly host praising God and saying,

14 "Glory to God in the highest,
 and on earth peace among those with whom he is pleased!"[a]

Righteousness comes from Christ as He is born into this world. The two words that are used there are joy and peace. In essence, He's come to bring joy and peace, and He's righteousness. Right there, at the very beginning, that's what He's come to do. He's come to bring joy, and He's come to bring shalom. He is righteousness.

The reaction by the heavenly hosts was great joy. Believe it, trust it now. Unfortunately, though, these verses are often misquoted. Yes, He's bringing peace on Earth—but not to everyone, only to whom His favor rests. This is an important clue. When reading that, our likely reaction is to question whether or not we are among those people. What does that mean for His favor coming to us? Is it possible for us to receive it? And what does that look like? It is not of the world but in Christ.

From the following three verses about Christ, what do they say about what He is? What is He bringing? What does that mean for us in our personal lives? Why is this important to us in our understanding of the Kingdom?

Read Isaiah 9:1–7:

For to Us a Child Is Born
9 [a] But there will be no gloom for her who was in anguish. In the former time he brought into contempt the land of Zebulun and the land of Naphtali, but in the latter time he has made glorious the way of the sea, the land beyond the Jordan, Galilee of the nations.[b]
2 [c] The people who walked in darkness
   have seen a great light;
those who dwelt in a land of deep darkness,
   on them has light shone.
3 You have multiplied the nation;
   you have increased its joy;
they rejoice before you
   as with joy at the harvest,
   as they are glad when they divide the spoil.
4 For the yoke of his burden,
   and the staff for his shoulder,
   the rod of his oppressor,
   you have broken as on the day of Midian.
5 For every boot of the tramping warrior in battle tumult
   and every garment rolled in blood
   will be burned as fuel for the fire.
6 For to us a child is born,
   to us a son is given;
and the government shall be upon[d] his shoulder,
   and his name shall be called[e]
Wonderful Counselor, Mighty God,
   Everlasting Father, Prince of Peace.

> [7] Of the increase of his government and of peace
>   there will be no end,
> on the throne of David and over his kingdom,
>   to establish it and to uphold it
> with justice and with righteousness
>   from this time forth and forevermore.
> The zeal of the Lord of hosts will do this.

____

____

____

____

____

Unto us, a child is born, and He's bringing His government—judgment based upon His righteousness and justice because of His righteousness. When we think of government, what does that imply? Rulership. He's bringing rulership to us and to life. It's going to be absolute justice, served by righteousness. He said He's going to be the Prince of Peace, bringing joy. These elements of the Kingdom are coming because of Christ. He's going to die for us and be resurrected. So, it begins and ends with Christ. He is righteousness, peace, and joy. If we're going to experience righteousness, peace, and joy, what needs to be true of us? We need to be with Him, receiving Him, living in Him.

Read Psalm 111:1–10:

Great Are the LORD'S Works

111 [a] Praise the LORD!
I will give thanks to the Lord with my whole heart,
   in the company of the upright, in the congregation.
[2] Great are the works of the LORD,
   studied by all who delight in them.
[3] Full of splendor and majesty is his work,
   and his righteousness endures forever.

> ⁴ He has caused his wondrous works to be remembered;
>   the LORD is gracious and merciful.
> ⁵ He provides food for those who fear him;
>   he remembers his covenant forever.
> ⁶ He has shown his people the power of his works,
>   in giving them the inheritance of the nations.
> ⁷ The works of his hands are faithful and just;
>   all his precepts are trustworthy;
> ⁸ they are established forever and ever,
>   to be performed with faithfulness and uprightness.
> ⁹ He sent redemption to his people;
>   he has commanded his covenant forever.
>   Holy and awesome is his name!
> ¹⁰ The fear of the LORD is the beginning of wisdom;
>   all those who practice it have a good understanding.
>   His praise endures forever!

He says that He's bringing righteousness, He's bringing wholeness, fullness of life, justice. He's bringing power, might, and strength with truth, verity, sureness. He remembers the Covenant. What does that mean? He promises that He's going to bless us to make us a blessing. That's first and foremost on His heart to deliver to us as His mission. He will command it. He will command it as we're walking in His Kingdom. *Commanding it* means what? It's going to happen. He's going to bring this about. Where? In reality, in our life, in the middle of a difficult place. He's going to command and deliver the Covenant to us so that we can enjoy living in and experiencing it.

Read John 10:10:

10 The thief comes only to steal, kill, and destroy. I came that they may have life and have it abundantly.

____

____

____

____

Jesus said, *I've come to give you life and give it to you super abundantly*. What life? The Covenant life. He's come to give us that in the middle of a difficult world—to give us super-abundant life, restoration, the life of the Kingdom.

From the following two verses, what statements did Jesus speak about His ministry—his purpose for coming to us? What do these mean in our personal lives? Why is this so significant to us as we learn to live in His Kingdom?

Read Luke 4:16–21:

Jesus Rejected at Nazareth
16 And he came to Nazareth, where he had been brought up. And as was his custom, he went to the synagogue on the Sabbath day, and he stood up to read. 17 And the scroll of the prophet Isaiah was given to him. He unrolled the scroll and found the place where it was written,

18 "The Spirit of the Lord is upon me,
    because he has anointed me
    to proclaim good news to the poor.
He has sent me to proclaim liberty to the captives
    and recovering of sight to the blind,
    to set at liberty those who are oppressed,
19 to proclaim the year of the Lord's favor."

> [20] And he rolled up the scroll and gave it back to the attendant and sat down. And the eyes of all in the synagogue were fixed on him. [21] And he began to say to them, "Today this Scripture has been fulfilled in your hearing."

____

____

____

____

____

His first public statement was to read Isaiah 61:1–4, and then He specifically said that this scripture has been fulfilled—in Him, right then. In other words, who fulfilled it? Christ, by coming to deliver the super-abundant life. When is this available to us? Now. Where? In His Kingdom.

Read Isaiah 61:1–4:

The Year of the Lord's Favor
61 The Spirit of the Lord God is upon me,
 because the Lord has anointed me
to bring good news to the poor;[a]
 he has sent me to bind up the brokenhearted,
to proclaim liberty to the captives,
 and the opening of the prison to those who are bound;[b]
[2] to proclaim the year of the Lord's favor,
 and the day of vengeance of our God;
 to comfort all who mourn;
[3] to grant to those who mourn in Zion—
 to give them a beautiful headdress instead of ashes,
the oil of gladness instead of mourning,
 the garment of praise instead of a faint spirit;
that they may be called oaks of righteousness,
 the planting of the Lord, that he may be glorified.[c]

> [4] They shall build up the ancient ruins;
>   they shall raise up the former devastations;
> they shall repair the ruined cities,
>   the devastations of many generations.

He said, *I've come to bring the good news.* Jesus was in the middle of this and kind of made a play on words here that He was in the middle of the Roman Empire. The Roman Empire had started around 60 B.C., and He was in the middle of that culture—being ruled by the Roman Empire. They conquered everybody. How? By force. They conquered all peoples by force and overwhelmed them—because they had a bigger army and were brilliant military people. As they conquered, they offered Pax Romana, the peace of Rome, but only once you surrendered and only if you promised not to cause any trouble. They would offer peace and protection, with the money you gave them, and they built cities, roads, and aqueducts. But if you caused any trouble, you would be arrested and killed. They enforced this by having military everywhere. Centurions, as they were called in the New Testament, stood on every corner. The Romans called Pax Romana the gospel, the good news. Here's the good news —you get peace from us, but only if you do it the way we want.

Here, Jesus is saying that the gospel is coming from Him and is about what He's ready to do—right now. It's good news, because everybody in the world has trouble, difficulty, great conflict, problems, things that are not working. The gospel says what? How about now? Are we willing to live in the Kingdom and receive what He's about ready to give us? There's no end to that, which means that regardless of the severity of where we are, the good news is what He can deliver to us now. When we experience that, we will then be the purveyor of the good news.

When people come to us, it will be our turn to ask them, *How about now, are you willing to go?*

The good news is He's going to bring us out of prison. He's going to give us healing for our broken heartedness, which might be why we're struggling. He's going to make joy in the place of heaviness. There will be mirth and gladness and there will be a great party. He's going to rebuild us. All this describes the super-abundant life—for us, now, even in the midst of this difficult world where we are constantly experiencing trouble.

In the following three verses, what does Christ say He desires to give us? What do these mean to us personally? What is important in understanding how we are to receive these?

Read John 14:25–28:

25 "These things I have spoken to you while I am still with you. 26 But the Helper, the Holy Spirit, whom the Father will send in my name, he will teach you all things and bring to your remembrance all that I have said to you. 27 Peace I leave with you; my peace I give to you. Not as the world gives do I give to you. Let not your hearts be troubled, neither let them be afraid. 28 You heard me say to you, 'I am going away, and I will come to you.' If you loved me, you would have rejoiced, because I am going to the Father, for the Father is greater than I.

He says He came to give us, deliver to us, hand over to us—peace. Shalom. He's come to give us favor. He says an interesting thing. He will not be giving as what? As the world gives, which is based on circumstances that are fleeting, where sometimes we receive it, and sometimes it is taken away. He said He's going to give it to us from the Spirit that we'll live in all the time. It will create what? Great joy. Because that's His heart for us. We need to let Him deliver it to us. What has to happen? We must have Him delivering that to us. It's not us getting it. It's receiving it from Him. See the difference?

Read John 17:9–26:

[9] I am praying for them. I am not praying for the world but for those whom you have given me, for they are yours. [10] All mine are yours, and yours are mine, and I am glorified in them. [11] And I am no longer in the world, but they are in the world, and I am coming to you. Holy Father, keep them in your name, which you have given me, that they may be one, even as we are one. [12] While I was with them, I kept them in your name, which you have given me. I have guarded them, and not one of them has been lost except the son of destruction, that the Scripture might be fulfilled. [13] But now I am coming to you, and these things I speak in the world, that they may have my joy fulfilled in themselves. [14] I have given them your word, and the world has hated them because they are not of the world, just as I am not of the world. [15] I do not ask that you take them out of the world, but that you keep them from the evil one.[a] [16] They are not of the world, just as I am not of the world. [17] Sanctify them[b] in the truth; your word is truth. [18] As you sent me into the world, so I have sent them into the world. [19] And for their sake I consecrate myself,[c] that they also may be sanctified[d] in truth.

[20] "I do not ask for these only, but also for those who will believe in me through their word, [21] that they may all be one, just as you, Father, are in me, and I in you, that they also may be in us, so that the world may believe that you have sent me. [22] The glory that you have given me I have given to them, that they may be one even as we are one, [23] I in them and you in me, that they may become perfectly one, so that the world may know that you sent me and loved them even as you loved me. [24] Father, I desire that they also, whom you have given me, may be with me where I am, to see my glory that you have given me because you loved me before the foundation of the world. [25] O righteous Father,

> even though the world does not know you, I know you, and these know that
> you have sent me. [26] I made known to them your name, and I will continue to
> make it known, that the love with which you have loved me may be in them,
> and I in them."

____

____

____

____

____

He said, *Father, You are righteous*. Who's righteous? The Father, the Son, the Holy Spirit. He said, *I'm praying that they become one as We are one*. He is praying that we will join Them and become united to Them—becoming one as They are one. By definition, when we join Him and become one with Him, we become what? Righteous. Why? Because we are joining Him, who is righteous, which He then gives that righteousness to us.

He has done this so that His joy may go into us and be fulfilled. It is rejoicing. Everything is thriving and going well for us. We are rejoicing exceedingly. May that be true? He's praying that would be true of us as we become one. He says something important—this happens through His speaking truth. The word. The word sanctifies. Sanctify means made righteous.

So, He's going to give us His joy through speaking His word that we will receive, which is Spirit, which is joy, which is peace, and we will become righteous. How will this happen? By walking with Him, being unified with Him, receiving His word. That's His purpose. His mission is to deliver the Covenant, deliver peace, to restore our life and to have us experience, not just learn about, but experience peace, righteousness, and joy.

Read John 15:1–11:

I Am the True Vine

15 "I am the true vine, and my Father is the vinedresser. [2] Every branch in me that does not bear fruit he takes away, and every branch that does bear fruit he prunes, that it may bear more fruit. [3] Already you are clean because of the word that I have spoken to you. [4] Abide in me, and I in you. As the branch cannot bear fruit by itself, unless it abides in the vine, neither can you, unless you abide in me. [5] I am the vine; you are the branches. Whoever abides in me and I in him, he it is that bears much fruit, for apart from me you can do nothing. [6] If anyone does not abide in me he is thrown away like a branch and withers; and the branches are gathered, thrown into the fire, and burned. [7] If you abide in me, and my words abide in you, ask whatever you wish, and it will be done for you. [8] By this my Father is glorified, that you bear much fruit and so prove to be my disciples. [9] As the Father has loved me, so have I loved you. Abide in my love. [10] If you keep my commandments, you will abide in my love, just as I have kept my Father's commandments and abide in his love. [11] These things I have spoken to you, that my joy may be in you, and that your joy may be full.

____

____

____

____

Abiding is choosing to remain as a branch connected to the vine, choosing to walk with Him, be with Him, stay connected to Him. The life comes from Him—apart from us. He says we can do what? Nothing. None of this will occur, which explains why people aren't experiencing righteousness, peace, and joy—they're actually outside the Kingdom, doing it on their own in the flesh. When we live in the Kingdom, abiding, we will receive His joy. Christ says that He wants His joy to be in us and our joy to overflow—super-abundantly overflow—so that we can't contain it. And we'll experience it as real joy. It's not a religious joy. No, it's real joy where we are really excited and really fulfilled because we are living the life of God. It's a true joy. The joy is a true emotion that we actually experience, and it's not dependent on circumstance.

LESSON 1:
WHAT IS THE KINGDOM AND THE PROMISED LIFE OF THE KINGDOM?

What does God say about all His paths? Knowing that we will experience difficulty and trouble, why is this important to us? How then shall we expect the experience of our path to be? Why?

Read Psalm 16:7–11:

[7] I bless the LORD who gives me counsel;
   in the night also my heart instructs me.[a]
[8] I have set the LORD always before me;
   because he is at my right hand, I shall not be shaken.
[9] Therefore my heart is glad, and my whole being[b] rejoices;
   my flesh also dwells secure.
[10] For you will not abandon my soul to Sheol,
   or let your holy one see corruption.[c]
[11] You make known to me the path of life;
   in your presence there is fullness of joy;
   at your right hand are pleasures forevermore.

____

____

____

____

____

He says that when we walk with Him, our paths are going to be what? Pleasant, sweet, lovely, agreeable, life. Where is that path? In the world. What's along that path? Difficulty, trouble, and adversity. But He says, He will plow through it. He will show us how to live in it so that as we're experiencing it, we know that He's going to resolve this. Then He says that He is going to give you *great joy*. Mirth, gaiety, excitement. He wants to give that to us because on His path, what's going to happen? It's going to be pleasant. It will be joyful.

What does John the Baptist say about what is true about Christ? How are we to receive what Christ wishes to give to us? What then is important for us in our relationship with Christ?

Read John 3:27–36:

27 John answered, "A person cannot receive even one thing unless it is given him from heaven. 28 You yourselves bear me witness, that I said, 'I am not the Christ, but I have been sent before him.' 29 The one who has the bride is the bridegroom. The friend of the bridegroom, who stands and hears him, rejoices greatly at the bridegroom's voice. Therefore this joy of mine is now complete. 30 He must increase, but I must decrease."[a]

31 He who comes from above is above all. He who is of the earth belongs to the earth and speaks in an earthly way. He who comes from heaven is above all. 32 He bears witness to what he has seen and heard, yet no one receives his testimony. 33 Whoever receives his testimony sets his seal to this, that God is true. 34 For he whom God has sent utters the words of God, for he gives the Spirit without measure. 35 The Father loves the Son and has given all things into his hand. 36 Whoever believes in the Son has eternal life; whoever does not obey the Son shall not see life, but the wrath of God remains on him.

John makes a couple of interesting statements. He says, *You're not going to receive any of this unless it's given to you from God, from heaven*. In other words, we can't get this on our own. There's a definition of the Kingdom—if we're trying to get this on our own, we're not in the Kingdom so we can't do it, it's not possible. It has to be delivered to us. It has to be given to us. John says, *I'm not the Christ, because the only one who can give it to you is Christ. I'm the friend*. He gives the analogy of the bridegroom with his attendants—his best friends—the ones who are privileged, who get to stand next to the bridegroom. If we stand next to the bridegroom, what happens? Tremendous joy. Why? We get to rejoice in what He's doing and what He's saying and experiencing. We get to hear His voice. We are connected to Him and we are His friend. We are standing next to Him and He speaks truth to us. By His word (the Greek word, *Rhema*—the application of Biblical truth to us, personally), He's speaking it to us, and we are going to have great joy, learned by living in the truth. How do we do that? We stand next to the bridegroom, knowing that something spectacular is going to happen. Something spectacular will be given to us. We don't have to chase it. We have got to be with Him in the Kingdom. It's His Kingdom. If that's true, then where do we need to be? With Him, in His Kingdom, through our choice to join Him.

How does God deliver to us the abundant life? What is critical for us then to receive this? How?

Read 1 Kings 8:53–61; 65–66:

53 For you separated them from among all the peoples of the earth to be your heritage, as you declared through Moses your servant, when you brought our fathers out of Egypt, O Lord God."

Solomon's Benediction
54 Now as Solomon finished offering all this prayer and plea to the Lord, he arose from before the altar of the Lord, where he had knelt with hands outstretched toward heaven. 55 And he stood and blessed all the assembly of Israel with a loud voice, saying, 56 "Blessed be the Lord who has given rest to his people Israel, according to all that he promised. Not one word has failed of all his good promise, which he spoke by Moses his servant. 57 The Lord our God be with us, as he was with our fathers. May he not leave us or forsake us, 58 that he may incline our hearts to him, to walk in all his ways and to keep

> his commandments, his statutes, and his rules, which he commanded our fathers. [59] Let these words of mine, with which I have pleaded before the Lord, be near to the Lord our God day and night, and may he maintain the cause of his servant and the cause of his people Israel, as each day requires, [60] that all the peoples of the earth may know that the Lord is God; there is no other. [61] Let your heart therefore be wholly true to the Lord our God, walking in his statutes and keeping his commandments, as at this day."

He says the way He delivers it to us is by fulfilling His promises. What does that mean? The word for promise is what He speaks. He will speak to us. Rhema— His promise to us.

Solomon said, *We have followed You, and we've experienced that not one single word has failed. It's been fulfilled. Everything You said has happened*. Why? Because He spoke it. As He delivers righteousness, peace, and joy, it happens in reality, in the circumstances of our life. They had celebrations and they went away with great joy, saying, *Hallelujah. It's actually true*. They had experienced everything that God said, and they're celebrating. Yes, in our circumstances, we will experience difficulties, problems, big decisions that we cannot figure out. There might be an issue—something that just happened and it is hard. Our question must always be, *God, what do You have to say about that as I walk in the Kingdom?* The King can handle it. We can experience the Covenant life—the life He delivered by overcoming this circumstance and providing resolution. He does this for us personally, in our life. This happens: righteousness, peace, and joy in the Kingdom of God.

As we move into Lesson 2 of *Living in the Kingdom of God—Righteousness, Peace, and, Joy*, we learned that His Kingdom is the Kingdom of righteousness, peace, and joy in the Holy Spirit as stated in Romans 14:17. It's Christ Himself. He is peace. He is joy. He is righteousness. That's why He's come. He said, *My purpose is to deliver to you the Covenant. I'm going to bless you to make you a blessing. All My paths are pleasant and joyful and full of peace.* He wants to make things happen in our lives. He said, *I've come to give you life and give it to you super abundantly.* He described it as the good news, the gospel. It's always: How about now? No matter what we have going with all of our difficulties, problems, conflicts, He says, *I can deliver this now in the Kingdom of God.* He delivers it by speaking promises, by speaking His word, and fulfilling what He says. And the joy for us is that we get to experience that, and we begin to trust it. So, the question is: How does He bring this about in a real life?

In what way is God righteousness? What does that mean to us? How does He deliver righteousness to us? What then is important for us to receive it? Why?

> "He brings His righteousness to us. He does it by the way He created the world. How did He create the world? He spoke it into existence."

Read Psalm 33:1–6; 9–20:

The Steadfast Love of the LORD

33 Shout for joy in the LORD, O you righteous!
  Praise befits the upright.
2 Give thanks to the LORD with the lyre;
  make melody to him with the harp of ten strings!
3 Sing to him a new song;
  play skillfully on the strings, with loud shouts.
4 For the word of the LORD is upright,
  and all his work is done in faithfulness.
5 He loves righteousness and justice;
  the earth is full of the steadfast love of the LORD.

[6] By the word of the LORD the heavens were made,
  and by the breath of his mouth all their host.

[9] For he spoke, and it came to be;
  he commanded, and it stood firm.

[10] The LORD brings the counsel of the nations to nothing;
  he frustrates the plans of the peoples.

[11] The counsel of the LORD stands forever,
  the plans of his heart to all generations.

[12] Blessed is the nation whose God is the LORD,
  the people whom he has chosen as his heritage!

[13] The LORD looks down from heaven;
  he sees all the children of man;

[14] from where he sits enthroned he looks out
  on all the inhabitants of the earth,

[15] he who fashions the hearts of them all
  and observes all their deeds.

[16] The king is not saved by his great army;
  a warrior is not delivered by his great strength.

[17] The war horse is a false hope for salvation,
  and by its great might it cannot rescue.

[18] Behold, the eye of the LORD is on those who fear him,
  on those who hope in his steadfast love,

[19] that he may deliver their soul from death
  and keep them alive in famine.

[20] Our soul waits for the LORD;
  he is our help and our shield.

____

____

____

____

____

He says several things here. He is righteous. Justice is holiness—being righteousness. He brings His righteousness to us. He does it by the way He created the world. How did He create the world? He spoke it into existence. It's called ex-nihilo—meaning, out of nothing. He didn't take matter and reform it. He spoke things into existence, so the material is subordinate to the spiritual. What does that mean? When He speaks His word, He can change things, He can make things happen because it's all been created by Him speaking it, and therefore is subject to that. The implication is this: We have difficult circumstances, issues, things that are not working. We tend to look at these in the natural, trying to find resolution on our own. And, of course, a lot of times we get to a place where it doesn't look like it ever can be resolved. We figure it just can't get to a good solution. It's too tough. We can't figure it out. It's called being in a double bind, no matter which way we turn, there's no resolution and we are stuck. When we get stuck and can't figure out a resolution to our issues, what happens? We move ahead with what we think is best but are resigned to believing that since there is no way to solve the issue, it is just going to be a continued problem that we are going to have to live with. He says, *If you allow Me, I'll speak to it and change it*. Why? Because He can. That's how the world was created. He says, *My words will be fulfilled. If you have a heart to receive it, My words will be fulfilled, and you can rejoice and have joy. You'll have great mirth in experiencing what I'm going to deliver to you*. Why? Because He changed things. He resolved the circumstances for us. We want to know how He's going to do that for us, but He says it's going to be supernatural, so we would not to be able to understand it anyway. He's not telling us how; we just have to trust that He will do it.

From the following three sets of verses, what are the benefits to us living in His Kingdom? What do these mean to us practically? How are we to receive these?

> **Read Zechariah 8:11–23:**
>
> [11] But now I will not deal with the remnant of this people as in the former days, declares the LORD of hosts. [12] For there shall be a sowing of peace. The vine shall give its fruit, and the ground shall give its produce, and the heavens shall give their dew. And I will cause the remnant of this people to possess all these things. [13] And as you have been a byword of cursing among the nations, O house of Judah and house of Israel, so will I save you, and you shall be a blessing. Fear not, but let your hands be strong."

> [14] For thus says the Lord of hosts: "As I purposed to bring disaster to you when your fathers provoked me to wrath, and I did not relent, says the LORD of hosts, [15] so again have I purposed in these days to bring good to Jerusalem and to the house of Judah; fear not. [16] These are the things that you shall do: Speak the truth to one another; render in your gates judgments that are true and make for peace; [17] do not devise evil in your hearts against one another, and love no false oath, for all these things I hate, declares the LORD."
>
> [18] And the word of the LORD of hosts came to me, saying, [19] "Thus says the LORD of hosts: The fast of the fourth month and the fast of the fifth and the fast of the seventh and the fast of the tenth shall be to the house of Judah seasons of joy and gladness and cheerful feasts. Therefore, love truth and peace.
>
> [20] "Thus says the LORD of hosts: Peoples shall yet come, even the inhabitants of many cities. [21] The inhabitants of one city shall go to another, saying, 'Let us go at once to entreat the favor of the LORD and to seek the LORD of hosts; I myself am going.' [22] Many peoples and strong nations shall come to seek the LORD of hosts in Jerusalem and to entreat the favor of the LORD. [23] Thus says the LORD of hosts: In those days ten men from the nations of every tongue shall take hold of the robe of a Jew, saying, 'Let us go with you, for we have heard that God is with you.'"

____

____

____

____

____

He says, *My seed, My word will prosper.* What God speaks will be fulfilled. He will change the circumstances and resolve our issues. We can count on it. Our produce will thrive. Since Israel was an agricultural society, what was He saying? Their provision and their livestock were going to thrive. He is going to set them free financially in this process. When there is a heavy burden from financial pressure, He will give provision, plenty to live in freedom. We're not talking about wealth but about freedom as we normally live, where we normally live. Then He says, *The dew of heaven will come upon you.* What is the dew of heaven? The work of the anointing of the Holy Spirit. It'll come and refresh us, lead us, and guide us to what? Joy. Peace. As we then pursue and experience love, truth, and shalom and then celebrate that reality—what happens? Other people will desire to come and be with us. Not because of anything we did, but because they can see that God is with us. We're living in shalom, even though we have had issues and difficult circumstances. They see us experiencing God's righteousness, peace, and joy—and wish to experience this also. We will teach them about living in the Kingdom and being in Christ.

Read Psalm 21:1–7:

The King Rejoices in the LORD'S Strength
To the choirmaster. A Psalm of David.
21 O LORD, in your strength the king rejoices,
and in your salvation how greatly he exults!
[2] You have given him his heart's desire
and have not withheld the request of his lips. *Selah*
[3] For you meet him with rich blessings;
you set a crown of fine gold upon his head.
[4] He asked life of you; you gave it to him,
length of days forever and ever.
[5] His glory is great through your salvation;
splendor and majesty you bestow on him.
[6] For you make him most blessed forever;[a]
you make him glad with the joy of your presence.
[7] For the king trusts in the LORD,
and through the steadfast love of the Most High he shall not be moved.

The words *steadfast* love mean loyal to the Covenant—Covenant loyalty. Through His Covenant loyalty, we're going to experience great and mighty things. He says, *I'm going to give you a great salvation*. The word *salvation* means the wholeness, the welfare, our prosperity—meaning free, and experiencing joy for all that we have. As He delivers that to us, He wants us to live in honor, glory, and majesty. When we think of majesty, what does that entail? What does that imply? Grand, spectacular—more than we can imagine. God's path is majesty. There's something special about it. He gives us the privilege of receiving it and delivers things that are majestic. We get to experience the grandeur of it—to thrill our heart, and gain our heart's desire. He wants to thrill our heart with gladness as we are excited about His delivering the majestic—not that we chased it, but because God gave us this experience, and there's more coming. More excitement and grandeur.

Read Proverbs 10:28:

²⁸ The hope of the righteous brings joy,
    but the expectation of the wicked will perish.

What brings joy? Hope. What is hope? Something that's coming, even though we may not see it. It's confident expectation. He says, Hope brings righteousness and gladness—mirth. It is having confidence that something is going to happen. Hope brings joy. Why? He's going to deliver what He says. It's not a false hope. We will receive resolution for the things we are in the middle of, which guess what? We're always in the middle of. If we wait for everything to be resolved, how long are we going to be waiting? Forever, as we'll never get there. Rather, hope brings joy because we are confident it will be resolved—this time, the next time, and all the times after that.

What are the fruits of righteousness? What do these mean to us? What specifically is the way for us to receive these (what does He do that provides us this opportunity)? Why is this so important for those living in the Kingdom?

Read Isaiah 30:15–20:

[15] For thus said the LORD God, the Holy One of Israel,
"In returning[a] and rest you shall be saved;
    in quietness and in trust shall be your strength."
But you were unwilling, [16] and you said,
"No! We will flee upon horses";
    therefore you shall flee away;
and, "We will ride upon swift steeds";
    therefore your pursuers shall be swift.
[17] A thousand shall flee at the threat of one;
    at the threat of five you shall flee,
till you are left
    like a flagstaff on the top of a mountain,
    like a signal on a hill.

The LORD Will Be Gracious
[18] Therefore the LORD waits to be gracious to you,
    and therefore he exalts himself to show mercy to you.
For the LORD is a God of justice;
    blessed are all those who wait for him.

[19] For a people shall dwell in Zion, in Jerusalem; you shall weep no more. He will surely be gracious to you at the sound of your cry. As soon as he hears it, he answers you. [20] And though the LORD give you the bread of adversity and the water of affliction, yet your Teacher will not hide himself anymore, but your eyes shall see your Teacher.

____

____

____

____

____

What does He say? He's going to bring what? Fruit—and that fruit is righteousness, peace (shalom), and quietness through what? Trust. In the middle of the circumstances, He is bringing shalom, quietness, a peaceful rest so our soul can be undisturbed in the middle of disturbing circumstances. Why? Because He's going to deliver us. God speaks, and we will have righteousness, peace, and quietness. How does He overcome the opposition, the injustice, the things that are coming against us, our struggles?

How did Jehoshaphat approach working through a very difficult situation, thinking that the likely outcome was not going to be good? Why were these steps important, and how might we follow these steps in our difficult circumstances?

Read 2 Chronicles 20:1–30:

Jehoshaphat's Prayer

20 After this the Moabites and Ammonites, and with them some of the Meunites,[a] came against Jehoshaphat for battle. [2] Some men came and told Jehoshaphat, "A great multitude is coming against you from Edom,[b] from beyond the sea; and, behold, they are in Hazazon-tamar" (that is, Engedi). [3] Then Jehoshaphat was afraid and set his face to seek the Lord and proclaimed a fast throughout all Judah. [4] And Judah assembled to seek help from the LORD; from all the cities of Judah they came to seek the LORD.

[5] And Jehoshaphat stood in the assembly of Judah and Jerusalem, in the house of the LORD, before the new court, [6] and said, "O LORD, God of our fathers, are you not God in heaven? You rule over all the kingdoms of the nations. In your hand are power and might, so that none is able to withstand you. [7] Did you not, our God, drive out the inhabitants of this land before your people Israel, and give it forever to the descendants of Abraham your friend? [8] And they have lived in it and have built for you in it a sanctuary for your name, saying, [9] 'If disaster comes upon us, the sword, judgment,[c] or pestilence, or famine, we will stand before this house and before you—for your name is in this house—and cry out to you in our affliction, and you will hear and save.' [10] And now behold, the men of Ammon and Moab and Mount Seir, whom you would not let Israel invade when they came from the land of Egypt, and whom they avoided and did not destroy— [11] behold, they reward us by coming to drive us out of your possession, which you have given us to inherit. [12] O our God, will you

not execute judgment on them? For we are powerless against this great horde that is coming against us. We do not know what to do, but our eyes are on you."

[13] Meanwhile all Judah stood before the LORD, with their little ones, their wives, and their children. [14] And the Spirit of the Lord came[d] upon Jahaziel the son of Zechariah, son of Benaiah, son of Jeiel, son of Mattaniah, a Levite of the sons of Asaph, in the midst of the assembly. [15] And he said, "Listen, all Judah and inhabitants of Jerusalem and King Jehoshaphat: Thus says the Lord to you, 'Do not be afraid and do not be dismayed at this great horde, for the battle is not yours but God's. [16] Tomorrow go down against them. Behold, they will come up by the ascent of Ziz. You will find them at the end of the valley, east of the wilderness of Jeruel. [17] You will not need to fight in this battle. Stand firm, hold your position, and see the salvation of the LORD on your behalf, O Judah and Jerusalem.' Do not be afraid and do not be dismayed. Tomorrow go out against them, and the Lord will be with you."

[18] Then Jehoshaphat bowed his head with his face to the ground, and all Judah and the inhabitants of Jerusalem fell down before the LORD, worshiping the LORD. [19] And the Levites, of the Kohathites and the Korahites, stood up to praise the LORD, the God of Israel, with a very loud voice.

[20] And they rose early in the morning and went out into the wilderness of Tekoa. And when they went out, Jehoshaphat stood and said, "Hear me, Judah and inhabitants of Jerusalem! Believe in the Lord your God, and you will be established; believe his prophets, and you will succeed." [21] And when he had taken counsel with the people, he appointed those who were to sing to the Lord and praise him in holy attire, as they went before the army, and say,

"Give thanks to the LORD,
    for his steadfast love endures forever."

[22] And when they began to sing and praise, the Lord set an ambush against the men of Ammon, Moab, and Mount Seir, who had come against Judah, so that they were routed. [23] For the men of Ammon and Moab rose against the inhabitants of Mount Seir, devoting them to destruction, and when they had made an end of the inhabitants of Seir, they all helped to destroy one another.

The Lord Delivers Judah

[24] When Judah came to the watchtower of the wilderness, they looked toward the horde, and behold, there[e] were dead bodies lying on the ground; none had escaped. [25] When Jehoshaphat and his people came to take their spoil, they found among them, in great numbers, goods, clothing, and precious things,

> which they took for themselves until they could carry no more. They were three days in taking the spoil, it was so much. [26] On the fourth day they assembled in the Valley of Beracah,[f] for there they blessed the LORD. Therefore the name of that place has been called the Valley of Beracah to this day. [27] Then they returned, every man of Judah and Jerusalem, and Jehoshaphat at their head, returning to Jerusalem with joy, for the LORD had made them rejoice over their enemies. [28] They came to Jerusalem with harps and lyres and trumpets, to the house of the LORD. [29] And the fear of God came on all the kingdoms of the countries when they heard that the LORD had fought against the enemies of Israel. [30] So the realm of Jehoshaphat was quiet, for his God gave him rest all around.

____

____

____

____

____

In this story, all the nations surrounding Israel (today, this would be similar to Lebanon, Jordan, Egypt, Syria) decided to band together and get rid of Israel. They wanted to conquer them, so a great multitude is coming against Israel, in En Gedi—a valley desert place, south of Jerusalem. (Today, this would be a 90-minute drive from Jerusalem.) Not only do they have a plan to come against Israel, but they're already there. Here is the issue: It's not that we're going to have problems in the future, we already have problems now. They're ready to come after us right now. Generally speaking, who's most likely to win? The bigger army. They all banded together, have a lot more people than we do, and believe absolutely that they're going to defeat us. Jehoshaphat's first response is fear.

Is fear an acceptable response? Yes. He understood that this could carry a very negative consequence—death, conquering, the end of the nation. He did not deny the problem. Instead, he acknowledged it and said he was afraid.

What did he do next? He stayed in this place of the Kingdom. He said, _We have a big problem. It's real, it's severe, and the consequences as far as we can see, are going to be bad. And I am afraid. But we need to go to God. Let's gather together to seek God._ His first reaction isn't to try to figure it out on his own. He didn't consider fleeing or surrendering to avoid getting killed or asking God to just take care of it. What did he do instead? He seeks God to see what he has to say about the situation. Since he knows God's word (their bible at the time), he starts with what God has already said—the Covenant. *I've given you this land, I will bless you to make you a blessing. This is the inheritance you have. If you have troubles, I'll take care of it.*

Jehoshaphat said, *I'm coming back to this truth that You've written, help me to receive that.* How is this going to apply to us here today? We don't know what to do. God says: *I'll give you righteousness, peace, and joy in the middle of it because I'm going to deliver this and overcome the opposition.* Because Jehoshaphat admitted that he didn't know what to do about this particular situation, he sought God to speak His answer. He doesn't tell God to take care of it and let him know when it's done. No, he's got to be part of it, and it's got to apply to this particular situation.

What do you have? What do you have to do? Jehoshaphat said, *Father, we don't know. You said You will deliver the Covenant, and we have received that, but what do You have to say about this situation?* He says: *This battle is not yours, it's Mine, but you must go out to battle, and I'll tell you exactly where they're going to be. Go to this place. Arm up. Go as if you're going to battle, and when you get there, watch and see what I'm going to do.* He is going to take care of it, but there was this instruction that required his participation. He told them what to do. Do they believe it? Jehoshaphat said yes and then spoke to the people. Let's believe the prophets. What have the prophets told us about? The Covenant. Then believe God who now applies it specifically to us. He told us He will take care of it as we are called to come to this specific place. And if we believe that, we will see the deliverance of the Lord.

He said that as soon as they believed, what happened? God set the ambush, and they slaughtered each other. Now did Jehoshaphat have to fight at all? The battle was God's, and he had to do as instructed, but he did not have to fight the battle. The enemy gets defeated and God says, *Go, take their stuff.* What stuff? So much stuff, including gold, silver, jewelry, and arms, it took them a week to get it and take it back to Jerusalem. Why did the enemy have all that stuff with them? Since they had the superior army and were going to occupy Israel, they brought all their household belongings. They brought all their belongings because they were expecting to win. And God said, *Now that they came and were defeated, all these things are yours.* Think of the majesty of that—not only were they threatened with annihilation, with likely defeat, they got to see Him defeat the enemy as well as the grandeur of His majestic work. They went home with great joy, but they had also rejoiced prior to the battle. They were already celebrating the truth of what God had to say. Why could they do that before it even happens? Hope. Jehoshaphat knew it was going to be fulfilled. What is critical to understanding this? We have to hear what He has to say. Once we hear it, we can receive it and then can rejoice. We now have hope, the confidence that what He says will be fulfilled in our circumstances—and we experience righteousness, peace, and joy.

When we are faced with difficult circumstances, what are we to do? What does God promise to deliver? What does that mean for us as we face difficulties?

> **Read Jeremiah 33:3:**
>
> ³ Call to me and I will answer you and will tell you great and hidden things that you have not known.

____

____

____

____

____

What is it that we're supposed to do? Call to Him so He'll do what? He'll answer us and tell us what? Great and mighty things that we don't know. We are not to try to figure things out on our own—rather to call to Him and receive the great and supernatural things that He will reveal and speak to our situation.

In the following three sets of verses—since we are in a world full of troubles, what are we to understand about what Christ promises to us about these troubles? What shall we then expect to experience, and what shall we expect about Him resolving our troubles? Why is this important?

> **Read John 16:33:**
>
> [33] I have said these things to you, that in me you may have peace. In the world you will have tribulation. But take heart; I have overcome the world."

____

____

____

____

____

Jesus says that He's telling us these things so that we will have peace—shalom. In the world, we're going to have what? Tribulation, trouble; the word _trouble_ means pressure, a pressing together—oppression, affliction, distress. There's going to be pressure when we have trouble. What's the pressure? Things are really going to get difficult, and as far as we can see, it likely is not going to work out well and will cause us serious problems. And then we get anxious. When we're anxious, we're weighed down, burdened, exhausted. But Christ says to be of good cheer. Be joyful. Why? Because He says He overcame it. In other words, we will be victorious in this trouble because He is superior to that trouble. This is why He says in both the Old Testament and in the New Testament that nothing is too difficult for Him. Why not? Because all He has to do is speak His answer, and it will be fulfilled. He's superior to all things, and it is why we are to receive and live in peace—shalom. What are we to do? Be of good cheer. He has actually overcome it already (past tense). We are to walk into it and enjoy the journey.

Read Psalm 32:6–11:

6 Therefore let everyone who is godly
  offer prayer to you at a time when you may be found;
surely in the rush of great waters,
  they shall not reach him.
7 You are a hiding place for me;
  you preserve me from trouble;
  you surround me with shouts of deliverance. *Selah*
8 I will instruct you and teach you in the way you should go;
  I will counsel you with my eye upon you.
9 Be not like a horse or a mule, without understanding,
  which must be curbed with bit and bridle,
  or it will not stay near you.
10 Many are the sorrows of the wicked,
  but steadfast love surrounds the one who trusts in the Lord.
11 Be glad in the LORD, and rejoice, O righteous,
  and shout for joy, all you upright in heart!

____

____

____

____

____

When we are in trouble, we are called to shout for joy—gladness—have gladness while we're in the middle of the trouble. Why? He will instruct us on how to let Him fulfill the issue that we have while we're in the Kingdom of God. He will instruct us by showing us how to walk, He will teach us how that works, and He will guide us by giving His counsel and process into the solution.

> **Read John 16:13–15:**
>
> [13] When the Spirit of truth comes, he will guide you into all the truth, for he will not speak on his own authority, but whatever he hears he will speak, and he will declare to you the things that are to come. [14] He will glorify me, for he will take what is mine and declare it to you. [15] All that the Father has is mine; therefore I said that he will take what is mine and declare it to you.

____

____

____

____

____

The Holy Spirit is going to guide us into all truth and tell us of things to come. *Here's what I speak to this. Here's My instruction. I'm going to transfer all that's of Christ to you, which are:* righteousness, peace, and joy. How does He guide us? Listen carefully to whatever He says and walk with Him along His path.

Why do people choose to follow guides? Guides know more than us. A guide says: *Come with me. Let me explain some things. I'll instruct you. I'll teach you. I'll show you.* And we do what? Ask questions. What about this? What do you have to say about this? God says: *Let Me give you an instruction. I'll tell you where to go. Walk into My resolution.* Think about how simple this is. We have a problem. Who can solve it? The King. Where is it solved? In the Kingdom. Where do we need to be? In the Kingdom. How? By letting Him guide us into the resolution. A real resolution. Not hypothetical. True resolution, which is why in times of trouble we are called to go to Gladness—it will be resolved, and we can trust it. It's a learning process. Let Him teach us and walk us into His resolution. He's the one who's guiding us—stay with Him. Go to gladness because He will resolve our issue, and we can count on this happening.

As we finish this second lesson, we just learned that God says: My heart is to deliver to you the Covenant, the peace, the shalom, righteousness. And I am delivering it to you by what I speak. My words will fulfill itself. I will guide you—stay with Me so I can do it. And we learn this is absolute—our belief, the hope, the confidence, the joy comes because we know that this will be so in our life. Whatever issue we have, whatever problem, whatever offense, God says: Come to Me and let Me resolve it. I'll speak to it. You will receive instruction. Let Me guide you. Stay with Me and let Me fulfill it.

> "He wants to restore through the good news, which means: How about now?"

We're headed into Lesson 3 of the course: *Living in the Kingdom of God—Righteousness, Peace, and Joy*. We've learned that Christ is righteousness, peace, and joy. It's all about receiving His life, being with Him, walking with Him. He says, *My purpose is to deliver the Covenant—bless you, to make you a blessing, to give you super-abundant life*. He wants to restore through the good news, which means: How about now? We can do it now—the beautiful things of life amongst the difficulties that we have. Are we going to have difficulties? Yes, He said, *In the world, you're going to have tribulation, but I've overcome it—start to live there and receive the joy, the hope, the expectation that I am going to resolve it. You can have joy and peace and righteousness in the middle of the trouble*. Why? Because He's going to resolve it. When we have trouble, if we're living in the Kingdom of God, we go to the King and ask what He has to say about our situation? What of Your power is going to overcome this? And then He speaks specifically as He asks us to walk in His ways, follow His instructions, be guided, stay with it until we experience it, and because we experience it, we rejoice.

What are the benefits of living in His Kingdom? What do each of these mean for us personally? Why is this so important to how we live?

Read Psalm 103:1–5:

Bless the LORD, O My Soul
Of David.
103 Bless the LORD, O my soul,
   and all that is within me,
   bless his holy name!
² Bless the LORD, O my soul,
   and forget not all his benefits,
³ who forgives all your iniquity,
   who heals all your diseases,
⁴ who redeems your life from the pit,
   who crowns you with steadfast love and mercy,
⁵ who satisfies you with good
   so that your youth is renewed like the eagle's.

____

____

____

____

____

Forget not the benefits of walking in the Kingdom. We don't need to live in guilt. We've been forgiven. He will heal our diseases now. He has forgiven our iniquities. Intellectually, we might understand it, but we don't tend to live it out. Why? We tend to live in guilt. We made a mistake. We have done things and are trying to resolve the issues. We want to do better, but we cannot and find ourselves stuck in a *woe is me* pattern. We think we are awful, and we can't get over the circumstances—so we have difficulty receiving true forgiveness and then forgiving ourselves.

He further says that He heals all our diseases. This is most difficult to understand and to believe because it seems this is not so. We see a lot of people who never get healed, so we figure this can't really be true. But because He did speak it (all scripture is God breathed), He asks if we have a heart to come and learn of this, to be guided into the truth of it.

He then says: He will heal us from our patterns, from the pit. We have patterns that are destructive—patterns of how we respond to situations. This response triggers a negative effect and the situation can escalate, causing worry, fear, anger, etc. We have an enemy who has been reinforcing our responses ever since we were kids. Once we are triggered, we typically think we can fix the problem, but God says that we can't fix that problem because there's something deeper going on inside of us about what we believe and how we respond. He has to heal that, not manage it, because if we still believed, we could manage it for a while. But what would happen? We would go back to the pattern. We'd give up on staying in the Kingdom. But God says He will heal us of that destructive pattern, not manage it. He will heal us at the root level of it, and He will transform us. And this results in a beautiful life with God: He will satisfy our life with good things, and He'll renew our youth—like an eagle soaring. We'll be soaring, we'll be free, we'll be experiencing the joy of that. Let Him do that because He wants to heal this deep pattern.

For us to enjoy the benefits of the Kingdom, where must we be? What does that mean to us personally? Why is that so important?

Read Isaiah 35:1–10:

The Ransomed Shall Return

35 The wilderness and the dry land shall be glad;
  the desert shall rejoice and blossom like the crocus;
² it shall blossom abundantly
  and rejoice with joy and singing.
The glory of Lebanon shall be given to it,
  the majesty of Carmel and Sharon.
They shall see the glory of the Lord,
  the majesty of our God.
³ Strengthen the weak hands,
  and make firm the feeble knees.
⁴ Say to those who have an anxious heart,
  "Be strong; fear not!
Behold, your God
  will come with vengeance,
with the recompense of God.
  He will come and save you."
⁵ Then the eyes of the blind shall be opened,
  and the ears of the deaf unstopped;
⁶ then shall the lame man leap like a deer,
  and the tongue of the mute sing for joy.
For waters break forth in the wilderness,
  and streams in the desert;
⁷ the burning sand shall become a pool,
  and the thirsty ground springs of water;
in the haunt of jackals, where they lie down,
  the grass shall become reeds and rushes.
⁸ And a highway shall be there,
  and it shall be called the Way of Holiness;
the unclean shall not pass over it.
  It shall belong to those who walk on the way;
  even if they are fools, they shall not go astray.[a]

> 9 No lion shall be there,
>   nor shall any ravenous beast come up on it;
> they shall not be found there,
>   but the redeemed shall walk there.
> 10 And the ransomed of the LORD shall return
>   and come to Zion with singing;
> everlasting joy shall be upon their heads;
>   they shall obtain gladness and joy,
>   and sorrow and sighing shall flee away.

____

____

____

____

God is majestic. God is glorious. God is all powerful. What does He say He'll do there? Transform, deliver us from the wilderness. What is the wilderness? Wilderness is dryness. Things aren't working. We are not getting any vitality. He says He is going to restore that and bring us back to wholeness. He's going to give us sight. He is going to give us light. He is going to restore us from our heaviness. He is going to place us upon His highway—a highway of holiness. In order to experience this, we have to be where? On the highway. He wants us to join Him on His highway where it is easier, smoother, and much faster. We don't stop. It's smooth and straight. If we live in His Kingdom, it'll be much easier, and we'll enjoy being on that highway. He will restore us. He will take the things that are burdening us because of our destructive patterns, and He'll restore them. We will then have joy and gladness. In Hebrew, joy is rejoicing, and gladness is the aspect of it thrilling our heart, the reason we're seeing things not just managed but truly transformed. And now we are free of it.

What does God promise us since much of our lives has been difficult, with much being lost or ruined? What does that mean to how we view our current circumstances? Why is this important?

Read Joel 2:19–32:

19 The LORD answered and said to his people,
"Behold, I am sending to you
    grain, wine, and oil,
    and you will be satisfied;
and I will no more make you
    a reproach among the nations.
20 "I will remove the northerner far from you,
    and drive him into a parched and desolate land,
his vanguard[a] into the eastern sea,
    and his rear guard[b] into the western sea;
the stench and foul smell of him will rise,
    for he has done great things.
21 "Fear not, O land;
    be glad and rejoice,
    for the LORD has done great things!
22 Fear not, you beasts of the field,
    for the pastures of the wilderness are green;
the tree bears its fruit;
    the fig tree and vine give their full yield.
23 "Be glad, O children of Zion,
    and rejoice in the LORD your God,
for he has given the early rain for your vindication;
    he has poured down for you abundant rain,
    the early and the latter rain, as before.
24 "The threshing floors shall be full of grain;
    the vats shall overflow with wine and oil.
25 I will restore[c] to you the years
    that the swarming locust has eaten,
the hopper, the destroyer, and the cutter,
    my great army, which I sent among you.
26 "You shall eat in plenty and be satisfied,
    and praise the name of the LORD your God,

> who has dealt wondrously with you.
> And my people shall never again be put to shame.
> [27] You shall know that I am in the midst of Israel,
>   and that I am the LORD your God and there is none else.
> And my people shall never again be put to shame.
>
> The LORD Will Pour Out His Spirit
> [28] [d] "And it shall come to pass afterward,
>   that I will pour out my Spirit on all flesh;
> your sons and your daughters shall prophesy,
>   your old men shall dream dreams,
>   and your young men shall see visions.
> [29] Even on the male and female servants
>   in those days I will pour out my Spirit.
>
> [30] "And I will show wonders in the heavens and on the earth, blood and fire and columns of smoke. [31] The sun shall be turned to darkness, and the moon to blood, before the great and awesome day of the Lord comes. [32] And it shall come to pass that everyone who calls on the name of the LORD shall be saved. For in Mount Zion and in Jerusalem there shall be those who escape, as the LORD has said, and among the survivors shall be those whom the LORD calls.

____

____

____

____

____

He says He knows we've lost this. Things have been ruined. What will He do? He will restore it. That word *restore* is shalom. He's going to restore it back to the favor that He had in mind. And He described it in significant detail—we're going to have great freedom because of what He is doing to restore—we will rejoice; we'll be celebrating because of what He does. But also while He is doing it so we can experience shalom.

Yes, we've lost things—maybe financial, time, or relationship. Whatever it was, it is not there anymore. God says He can restore it to us now, when we're in the middle of it—perhaps not the way or how we thought it should be restored but in the grand way that only God can restore. He is going to give us the Covenant. He is going to bless us to give it away—and He will bless those who bless us and curse those who curse us. We can still live in righteousness, peace, and joy if we come with Him. Why? We can believe and expect it. We are going to be restored now. We don't know how, and it hasn't happened yet. And as far as we are concerned, it doesn't really make any sense, but He's going to restore this. And we can trust it and believe it, because He says—in His Kingdom, He will restore—give us shalom, favor.

From the following three sets of verses—to live in the Kingdom, what are our current responses to the life of God? What then shall we expect, and what will we bear witness to? Why? What then is the significance of that?

Read 1 Chronicles 16:7–17:

7 Then on that day David first appointed that thanksgiving be sung to the Lord by Asaph and his brothers.

David's Song of Thanks
8 Oh give thanks to the LORD; call upon his name;
   make known his deeds among the peoples!
9 Sing to him, sing praises to him;
   tell of all his wondrous works!
10 Glory in his holy name;
   let the hearts of those who seek the LORD rejoice!
11 Seek the LORD and his strength;
   seek his presence continually!
12 Remember the wondrous works that he has done,
   his miracles and the judgments he uttered,
13 O offspring of Israel his servant,
   children of Jacob, his chosen ones!
14 He is the LORD our God;
   his judgments are in all the earth.
15 Remember his covenant forever,
   the word that he commanded, for a thousand generations,
16 the covenant that he made with Abraham,
   his sworn promise to Isaac,
17 which he confirmed to Jacob as a statute,
   to Israel as an everlasting covenant,

____

____

____

____

____

Go to thanksgiving. Go to praise. Think about His wondrous works. How could we think of wondrous works? We have to be in the Kingdom, experiencing them, and then we can share what we've seen happen. Wow. Look at that. We can share with others all that God has done because we are in the Kingdom, experiencing His wondrous works. Keep remembering the Covenant—the activity of the Covenant in our life. By looking at the past, reading old journals, remembering, we can bring to mind all the glorious works that He's already done. Remember, in this situation, He's going to restore us. He is going to fix our problems. Remember that the Covenant is so. Remember the essence of the Covenant in all the situations we are in. Remember that we are on the path of the Kingdom. We are in the Kingdom of God. When we see wondrous work, we should share that with others, because just as it thrills our heart, it will also thrill their heart. Why? Because it reinforces that this life is true, and it gives another point of proof that this life is true.

Read 1 Chronicles 16:27–36:

27 Splendor and majesty are before him;
   strength and joy are in his place.
28 Ascribe to the LORD, O families of the peoples,
   ascribe to the LORD glory and strength!
29 Ascribe to the LORD the glory due his name;
   bring an offering and come before him!
Worship the Lord in the splendor of holiness;[a]
30   tremble before him, all the earth;
   yes, the world is established; it shall never be moved.
31 Let the heavens be glad, and let the earth rejoice,
   and let them say among the nations, "The LORD reigns!"
32 Let the sea roar, and all that fills it;
   let the field exult, and everything in it!

> 33 Then shall the trees of the forest sing for joy
>   before the LORD, for he comes to judge the earth.
> 34 Oh give thanks to the Lord, for he is good;
>   for his steadfast love endures forever!
>
> 35 Say also:
> "Save us, O God of our salvation,
>   and gather and deliver us from among the nations,
> that we may give thanks to your holy name
>   and glory in your praise.
> 36 Blessed be the LORD, the God of Israel,
>   from everlasting to everlasting!"
>
> Then all the people said, "Amen!" and praised the Lord.

____

____

____

____

____

Praise the Lord as we experience His everlasting love—in the Hebrew these words mean Covenant loyalty. Trust that God is loyal to the Covenant and that it will be given to us all the time, every time—and we will experience His splendor, majesty, strength, and gladness—in His place. Where is that? His Kingdom, where there is the King and the King reigns. Where we recognize that He reigns, He is superior, and He can make things happen. We will let Him be the King, and we'll live with Him because He reigns.

As we experience His glory, majesty, strength, and gladness—in that place, we will ascribe glory to God. Why will we give glory to God and not to ourselves? Because we didn't do it. He did. He is the One who has done the supernatural—not us. If we're giving glory to God, it means that He has done wondrous works—miracles. We are ascribing glory to Him, which is His purpose of delivering the beautiful Kingdom to us so that we enjoy it, receive it, give it away, and what else? Glorify God.

Read Philippians 4:4–9:

4 Rejoice in the Lord always; again I will say, rejoice. 5 Let your reasonableness[a] be known to everyone. The Lord is at hand; 6 do not be anxious about anything, but in everything by prayer and supplication with thanksgiving let your requests be made known to God. 7 And the peace of God, which surpasses all understanding, will guard your hearts and your minds in Christ Jesus.

8 Finally, brothers, whatever is true, whatever is honorable, whatever is just, whatever is pure, whatever is lovely, whatever is commendable, if there is any excellence, if there is anything worthy of praise, think about these things. 9 What you have learned[b] and received and heard and seen in me—practice these things, and the God of peace will be with you.

____

____

____

____

____

He says to rejoice. Let the Spirit give us His joy. How often? In everything. Yes, we have issues, problems, difficult things going on, but rejoice. He says to let our requests be made known. We have learned about seeking God and His solutions. What is His will for this situation? What does He have to say about this? It is not, *God, take care of this. Here's our wish list. See You later.* Rather, our request should be what? *God, we need to hear what You have to say about this*—and when we do that, He said the shalom of God will guard our heart. Think about that. While we're in the middle of the problem, we go to God. Why are we going to have the shalom of God? Because we know that He can resolve whatever issue we have. He can speak it and give us shalom right now. If something hasn't been resolved yet, He merely has to speak it so. And now we have shalom. It's going to happen. We go to Him to get the answer, and He's going to resolve it. We can trust it.

He says that the key is to keep our mind on Him and things that are true, pure, honorable, and excellent. In other words, don't think about the issue or how unfortunate we think we are or question why? Why? Why? Think of the majesty that He is bringing because we are with Him. He is going to resolve this. Think about that. This replaces anxiousness with trust, peace, and joy. Anxiousness is the opposite of thanking and trusting God. We are dwelling on things that are not good, that are not commendable, that are not excellent, that are not praiseworthy. We are dwelling on the opposite. Why does that make us anxious? Just by its very nature, it's against the nature of God. We've gone to the natural, and in the natural, what do we conclude about this problem? We can't fix it, and we don't know what else to do—this isn't going to work out. So we go to fear and anxiety. As far as we can see, this isn't going to work out. And then we think about it and stew on it and cogitate on it and obsess over it. It oppresses us. He says to go to His presence with thanksgiving, praise, and worship, seeking Him in His presence.

To live in the Kingdom and not be obligated to live in the world, in the flesh, what is necessary on our part? How do we fulfill this? What then is the promise given to us if we fulfill our part? Why is this important to us?

Read Romans 8:5; 12–17:

[5] For those who live according to the flesh set their minds on the things of the flesh, but those who live according to the Spirit set their minds on the things of the Spirit.

Heirs with Christ
[12] So then, brothers,[a] we are debtors, not to the flesh, to live according to the flesh. [13] For if you live according to the flesh you will die, but if by the Spirit you put to death the deeds of the body, you will live. [14] For all who are led by the Spirit of God are sons[b] of God. [15] For you did not receive the spirit of slavery to fall back into fear, but you have received the Spirit of adoption as sons, by whom we cry, "Abba! Father!" [16] The Spirit himself bears witness with our spirit that we are children of God, [17] and if children, then heirs—heirs of God and fellow heirs with Christ, provided we suffer with him in order that we may also be glorified with him.

As we learned in Philippians, we are to set our mind on the things of the Spirit. What do You have to say? What's Your perspective on this? We have a heart to do just that. Then He says, we're not obligated to live in the flesh outside the Kingdom, but rather to live in the Kingdom and be led by the Spirit, the King. If He's leading, what are we doing? We are following. And if we're following, by definition, we're willing to be led. Why would we be willing to be led by the King? Because He has the supernatural power to take care of our issue, He has the solutions. He not only knows the answer, but He can also perform the answer. He's also loving, and He's good. We can trust Him. He has a heart for us. He loves us. He cares about us. We are His children. He is going to confirm that we are His children.

If we're going to walk in the Kingdom, we have to be in a position where we're willing to be led by the King. And if He's the King, then we aren't the King. What does the King do? He gives His life for us. We have to follow His life as He can't deliver it to us when we're not in the Kingdom. If we're being led, we have a heart to hear what He has to say. What's His promise? What's His instruction? What's His guidance? We must follow Him into the answer. We need to be willing to do that. Why? Because it's best and none better. We have to surrender our will to His will.

Review the following three sets of verses. In life many things do not make sense; and we are experiencing circumstances that are difficult to understand and work through. How are we to approach God regarding these? What does He promise? What then does that mean to us and how we live?

Read 1 Kings 10:1–9:

The Queen of Sheba
10 Now when the queen of Sheba heard of the fame of Solomon concerning the name of the LORD, she came to test him with hard questions. ² She came to Jerusalem with a very great retinue, with camels bearing spices and very much gold and precious stones. And when she came to Solomon, she told him all that was on her mind. ³ And Solomon answered all her questions; there was nothing hidden from the king that he could not explain to her. ⁴ And when the queen of Sheba had seen all the wisdom of Solomon, the house that he had built, ⁵ the food of his table, the seating of his officials, and the attendance of his servants, their clothing, his cupbearers, and his burnt offerings that he offered at the house of the Lord, there was no more breath in her.

> [6] And she said to the king, "The report was true that I heard in my own land of your words and of your wisdom, [7] but I did not believe the reports until I came and my own eyes had seen it. And behold, the half was not told me. Your wisdom and prosperity surpass the report that I heard. [8] Happy are your men! Happy are your servants, who continually stand before you and hear your wisdom! [9] Blessed be the LORD your God, who has delighted in you and set you on the throne of Israel! Because the LORD loved Israel forever, he has made you king, that you may execute justice and righteousness."

____

____

____

____

____

The Queen of Sheba represents us. Solomon, who received his wisdom from God, represents God. She brought with her every hard question that she had on her mind. As the queen, she had seen and experienced a lot and had a number of questions, hard questions. Her questions covered a number of difficult things, and she asked them all. What did he do? He answered every one of them. Not a single one went unanswered. He even took her breath away as his answers were so overwhelming that they literally rendered her speechless. She was in awe. The majesty—she observed it. She said that it wasn't just hollow information but she saw it in reality right in front of her. It's true. Wow. Look at that. Majesty. We see something. We observe something. Our heart is different. He says if we are going to surrender our will to Him, we will have a lot of questions—all the time because we're walking through a step-by-step process, so life will never be fully solved. Even with the current issue resolved, we will always have the next new thing that we have to deal with. So, we will always have questions, and they're tough because life is difficult. Thankfully, for every question we have, we can go to Him, ask Him what He thinks, and He will tell us the answer.

Read Proverbs 8:17–21; 32–35:

17 I love those who love me,
  and those who seek me diligently find me.
18 Riches and honor are with me,
  enduring wealth and righteousness.
19 My fruit is better than gold, even fine gold,
  and my yield than choice silver.
20 I walk in the way of righteousness,
  in the paths of justice,
21 granting an inheritance to those who love me,
  and filling their treasuries.

32 "And now, O sons, listen to me:
  blessed are those who keep my ways.
33 Hear instruction and be wise,
  and do not neglect it.
34 Blessed is the one who listens to me,
  watching daily at my gates,
  waiting beside my doors.
35 For whoever finds me finds life
  and obtains favor from the LORD,

____

____

____

____

____

If we don't seek wisdom, we are actually hurting ourselves. God is revealing that when we seek wisdom, He will give us honor and excellence. He says His path is a path of righteousness and justice. He will establish righteousness. It will be righteous. It will be just. He will resolve it. Stay with Him and we will see it. We will experience it. Don't worry. His path is righteousness—so stay on His path and we'll experience splendor and honor in abundance because He is going to give it to us.

How do we do that? Listen, watch, wait. What are we waiting for? We are waiting to hear what He has to say about this. We are listening and processing together. We are watching what happens next. Something will happen. Something will be given. Something will be revealed. Some new piece of information will be revealed because we're alert and we're watching. We are waiting. The word *wait* means to dance with Him. Do not stop. Just keep walking on the path and dancing with Him as He is going to give us the answer that we're seeking. We will hear it because we are listening. Listen, watch, and wait until the answer is clear. Think about the simplicity of walking with Him. What does that imply? Movement. We are moving on a path, His path, where our steps are directed. He will show us the path. Stay with Him on the path. Walk with Him. He repeats that over and over again. Stay with Him where there is peace and joy, not anxiety and fear.

> **Read Matthew 6:33–34:**
>
> 33 But seek first the kingdom of God and his righteousness, and all these things will be added to you.
>
> 34 "Therefore do not be anxious about tomorrow, for tomorrow will be anxious for itself. Sufficient for the day is its own trouble.

____

____

____

____

____

We are to first and foremost seek what? The Kingdom. If we are seeking the Kingdom, we are also seeking the King and His righteousness. He is righteousness, so we seek Him to stay in the Kingdom and seek the answers from the King. If we do, what happens? All these things will be added unto us. What things? Whatever it is that we need. All the issues of life will be delivered to us. He will resolve our issues. He will restore. He will transform us. All of this will be given to us, delivered to us. What does that imply? We are the receiver. Where? In the Kingdom of God. By what? By seeking it and desiring it. We went after it, which is why He specifically makes that statement to seek the Kingdom. If we have to seek it, is it automatic? No. We have to understand this because a number of believers think everyone is already in the Kingdom. But this is not true. We've got to seek it. We've got to seek it by being led by the King.

As we conclude this lesson, we've seen some beautiful things. We have established that our role is to seek the Kingdom, surrender our will, be willing to go to truth, be willing to listen, watch, and wait to see Him deliver it. We can go to Him with all the difficult questions we have. He said He will answer them all, even our toughest ones. Stay with Him. Be led by Him. Be guided by Him. He will show us His path in the Kingdom. Move forward with Him, waiting—dancing—moving forward step by step by step as we stay with Him in the Kingdom. He says, He will fulfill it, and all these things will be given to us.

As we continue into Lesson 4 of our course, *Living in the Kingdom of God—Righteousness, Peace, and Joy*, we've spent time understanding that the Kingdom is righteousness, peace, and joy in the Holy Spirit. He's the King and our role is to surrender to that King—if we seek first the Kingdom and His righteousness, all these things will be given to us. It's really simple: If we're going to enjoy the Kingdom, which is a privilege, the things of our soul are transformed. The patterns that we fall into are not going to be managed. We're going to have them transformed. We're going to live with the expectation that He's going to deliver the Covenant, which is why He's come. He has come to give us life and give it to us super abundantly. He has come to restore the things that we have lost.

As we understand that, we're going to have to be in His Kingdom. To be in the Kingdom, we have to recognize Him as King, which means we surrender our will to Him and walk in His will, which we are seeking. He says we can ask Him all the tough questions and He says He will answer all of them and guide us and lead us into His will, which happens in the Kingdom of God. As we continue now in Lesson 4, the question here is, "How do we seek and live in the Kingdom?"

> "To be in the Kingdom, we have to recognize Him as King, which means we surrender our will to Him and walk in His will, which we are seeking."

To live in the Kingdom, how are we to pray? What are we to ask for? What shall we expect? What does that mean to how we live? Why?

Read John 16:23–24:

[23] In that day you will ask nothing of me. Truly, truly, I say to you, whatever you ask of the Father in my name, he will give it to you. [24] Until now you have asked nothing in my name. Ask, and you will receive, that your joy may be full.

____

____

____

____

____

He says, *Up until now, you haven't prayed anything in My name.* There's a really simple reason for that. Why not? The disciples did not have to pray, as they could just ask Him directly in the flesh. *Up until now, you have never understood real prayer. From this point forward, how do you pray? In My name. In essence, keep doing what you have been doing. You have been with Me. You ask Me questions. You talk to Me.*

As learned in Luke 10, we are to pray that Thy Kingdom come as it is in heaven. It's done perfectly there. So, by definition, He's saying two things. First, that we live where? In the Kingdom. And we have to ask for that. We've got to seek that; we've got to understand that it's not automatic. Secondly, we are to ask for His will to be done in the Kingdom. Now that we're in the Kingdom, ask for His will to be done. That's what the prayer is all about. So, He said from this point forward, we operate like we have been operating, but guess what? He is not going to be standing next to us. He is going to be where? He is going to be in us—to answer our questions and resolve our issues.

Further, *in His name* means something. We typically tack it on at the end of a prayer. God, would you? Would you? Would you? In the name of Christ, Amen. As a Hebrew understood when God says, *In My name*, it is in His full character, His nature, His essence. When God told Moses to go to Pharaoh, Moses says, *Who shall I say sent me? God says: I am the I am. My name is the "I am."*

He continues throughout scripture where there are literally a hundred different names for God.

Anything we need, anything we have, He can deliver. He is everything, and He is going to demonstrate that to us step by step by step. If we need provision or are struggling financially, what would we like to know about His name? That He is the provider. If we're sick, He is the healer. If we are lost, He is the guide.

You see what He's saying is in His name. Everything. He is saying, *Learn My name, which is, "I am."* When we pray, what are we to do? He said to do what we have been doing, which was to ask Him questions. *How do we do this? How does this work? What do You have to say about that? God, we've got a problem here. How are You going to resolve this one?*

He ends the statement with, *If you learn to pray to Me, you're joy will be great—full.* What would bring joy to this process? Continuing to abide with Him—hearing His voice, following Him, and getting to be with Him, the One who is joy.

What happened when the disciples were discouraged and afraid? What did that mean to them? Why? What then is important for us to experience the life of the Kingdom?

> **Read John 20:19–21:**
>
> Jesus Appears to the Disciples
> [19] On the evening of that day, the first day of the week, the doors being locked where the disciples were for fear of the Jews,[a] Jesus came and stood among them and said to them, "Peace be with you." [20] When he had said this, he showed them his hands and his side. Then the disciples were glad when they saw the Lord. [21] Jesus said to them again, "Peace be with you. As the Father has sent me, even so I am sending you."

____

____

____

____

____

The disciples were discouraged and fearful since their Messiah, Christ, had died, and they thought He was gone—dead and buried. Their hopes and dreams were shattered, and they thought that maybe He was not truly the Messiah, and that they had wasted their time. Jesus then shows up through the door. What's their immediate reaction? They were joyful. *Oh, hallelujah, this isn't over. Hallelujah, we get to be with You. Christ Himself was the joy.*

Christ also came to show His will, to resolve things, to demonstrate things, to live it. And we'll be joyful in the asking because we realize who we're talking to. We get to be together. We trust Him and we get to be with Him. And the joy that is Christ Himself is now ours.

As we seek God and His life for us, what role does scripture play? Why can we count on the application and power of this? What does that mean then for how we approach life issues? Why?

> **Read 2 Timothy 3:16–17:**
>
> [16] All Scripture is breathed out by God and profitable for teaching, for reproof, for correction, and for training in righteousness, [17] that the man of God[a] may be complete, equipped for every good work.

____

____

____

____

____

God understands that we will have lots of questions. We are to seek His will—what does He have to say about this? The starting point is the Word of God—logos. He has written (through speaking to the men who wrote it) truth. All scripture is inspired, breathed into the word by God. It is life. It is spirit and life. It is all true, and it is profitable for us. And it is available as a starting point. If we have an issue with a lawsuit, a conflict with a friend or spouse, or we've lost some money, how should we handle this? He said He has actually written about that. So, as we pursue truth and stay in the Kingdom, where should we go? Into God's Word. We are to search His Word to discover what He has to say about our situation. As we dialogue with Him to receive and understand His will, He will ask us if we believe it. This takes some time to process how it applies to us and to realize if we are experiencing this. We aren't to simply know about it, but we are to experience it.

As we receive the Word that God speaks to us, what can we understand about that Word to us? Why is that important for us and how we live? What is required then on our part?

> **Read 2 Corinthians 1:18–20:**
>
> [18] As surely as God is faithful, our word to you has not been Yes and No. [19] For the Son of God, Jesus Christ, whom we proclaimed among you, Silvanus and Timothy and I, was not Yes and No, but in him it is always Yes. [20] For all the promises of God find their Yes in him. That is why it is through him that we utter our Amen to God for his glory.

____

____

____

____

____

The promises of God are not Yes and No. They are all what? They are all yes, they are all true. So, as we're pursuing truth, we ask, *What do You have to say? What is Your promise to me?* He said they are not variable. They are not perhaps. They are not, *Well, some of you are lucky, and some of you aren't.* Or, *Some of it applies sometimes and other times not.* No, it's all true—there is absolutely no variation in Christ. If we're in Christ, we're living in the Kingdom of God. We have to be in the Kingdom because the promises are fulfilled in the Kingdom, not in the world.

Who is delivering the promise to us? Jesus Christ. It will be delivered when He speaks it to us. That's why our question in prayer is pure. *God, what do You have to say about this? It is not, We would like that promise, and we would like it applied to this situation, and we'd like it done in the way we think it should be done.*

All the promises are yes in Christ. Think about the simplicity of this. His promises have to be given. They have to be spoken. We have to seek what He has to say. He has to continue to be King, which will give us wisdom and insight. If we ask a pure question, *God, what have You to say about this?*, we will receive His answer. *Let Me guide you, let Me give you wisdom, let Me walk you through, let Me show you the answer.* All too often, we are asking the wrong question. This isn't about Him blessing our will, it's about us seeking His. We need to be pure and ask what He has to say about this. And He said, if we do, then we can be assured that when He says the promise, He's going to fulfill it. Our response is then to say what? Amen. What does amen mean? May it be complete—so be it. While we tend to look at amen as the end of a prayer— amen, it's over, done. But the Jewish understanding is much stronger. It means, *It's true. I've heard what You said. I understand it applies to me. I see how it applies to my situation and You have promised. So, therefore, may it please You to fulfill what You just said. So be it. It's a very strong statement. Amen. So be it.* Why? Because we've agreed with the promise. And if we agree with the promise by definition, what does that mean has happened? We've had to hear and we've cared to hear it. This is how it works. The Kingdom of God is letting Him be King with us believing it.

Abraham was described as a great man of faith. Was he always living by faith? What was necessary for him to become a great man of faith? How does God move us to being men and women of faith? How do we then receive that? Why?

Read Romans 4:17–21:

[17] as it is written, "I have made you the father of many nations"—in the presence of the God in whom he believed, who gives life to the dead and calls into existence the things that do not exist. [18] In hope he believed against hope, that he should become the father of many nations, as he had been told, "So shall your offspring be." [19] He did not weaken in faith when he considered his own body, which was as good as dead (since he was about a hundred years old), or when he considered the barrenness[a] of Sarah's womb. [20] No unbelief made him waver concerning the promise of God, but he grew strong in his faith as he gave glory to God, [21] fully convinced that God was able to do what he had promised.

Abraham believed God—but it took a while, and he made a lot of mistakes in the process. He laid with Hagar and had Ishmael, and he also tried to pass his wife off as his sister a couple of times. But he was fully persuaded, fully convinced that God would perform what? What He promised, what He said. God doesn't mind convincing us. He understands that's what it is going to take for the truth of what He says to become real, particularly for those who say they have never even experienced this fantastic abundant life. They don't understand what He's talking about, and they have their doubts. But, if we have a heart to seek God's will instead of our own, what will God do? He will persuade us.

Another great example that reflects this is when Jesus meets and calls His 12 disciples. Who were they? They were at the lower end of the caste system of Israeli fishermen. They were not religious leaders. They were tradesmen, workers without a lot of education or wisdom. They don't know much, particularly the things and supernatural life of God. God says to them, *Come and follow Me*, and then starts doing what? The supernatural stuff. But even in the third year of being together, He often said to them, *Ye of little faith, how long am I going to have to put up with your unbelief?* And they said, *Well, a little bit longer. But we're staying. We're going to stay with You.* They stayed with Him, and He persuaded them that what He had to say was true. As Acts came through the power of the Holy Spirit at Pentecost, they were completely persuaded.

It took three years for them to do it, but Jesus doesn't mind. He knows it's going to take us some time. It's not about jumping and leaping into it—rather, stay in the Kingdom, experience the Kingdom, believe the Kingdom. He says, *If you have a heart, come with Me, and I'll persuade you to believe what I have to say and that what I say is going to happen.* Let Him persuade us now.

To live in the Kingdom, we are called to go to unity. What exactly is that? Who is unity with? What is required for us to get to unity? What happens when we get to unity? Why? What then can we count on for all our life decisions and issues? Why?

Read Ephesians 4:1–6:

Unity in the Body of Christ
4 I therefore, a prisoner for the Lord, urge you to walk in a manner worthy of the calling to which you have been called, ² with all humility and gentleness, with patience, bearing with one another in love, ³ eager to maintain the unity of the Spirit in the bond of peace. ⁴ There is one body and one Spirit—just as

> you were called to the one hope that belongs to your call— [5] one Lord, one faith, one baptism, [6] one God and Father of all, who is over all and through all and in all.

He says to make every effort (the Greek word for *effort* means to work really, really, really, really, really hard) to go to unity with the Spirit. Your unity isn't with each other, per se—it's not negotiation. Rather, it is to give you a way for confirmation that you together are understanding God's will has been spoken to you, you have processed it, and have clarity as it applies to you and your life. He also says that He can get us there 100% of the time, all the time. Why? Because the Holy Spirit is within us, and within those with whom we are seeking God's will. We can and will get to unity with the Spirit because He will be telling the same thing to us individually. There is only one Spirit who will give the same information to everyone going to unity.

When we get to unity, we discover His will. As we are seeking His will together, we ask Him what He has to say to us. We ask what He is going to do. Then, together, we discuss what each is hearing and understanding, the perspective, insight, and wisdom—until we both or all (if inner circle of friends or family) get to unity and know God's will. We have not negotiated this, but rather, our spirit, which is in shalom—confirmed, in peace, feels good about this. If this has not happened yet, we must continue to seek and pay attention to the troubling lack of peace and lack of confirmation, as there is more to receive and understand. Trust the process and work really, really hard to receive and confirm unity in the Spirit.

As we experience disagreement (not unity), this is an indication that we are not there yet. Admit that we just don't know God's will yet but keep going. We know that God is going to get us there 100% of the time, all the time, if we have a heart to go. Everyone involved has to want God's will and be willing to continue until we receive the unity of the Spirit. There can be no pride or selfish resolve to go at it on our own. That is not unity with the Spirit.

The only question is, *Do we know God's will?* Either we do or we don't. It's a spiritual *Yes, we got there, or No, not quite. There's more information coming.* We help each other—spouse, friend, inner circle, small groups—with a willingness to respond to what others might be receiving. Maybe there is something else we ought to consider? Here's the truth, here's a new thought to ponder, and thus, our response should be to go and process that with God. If it's true, what will God do for us? He will confirm that the input is for us. *Yes, that's it!* or *No, that is not it. Don't go that way.* Instead, keep listening, keep processing, keep at it until we get confirmation through unity.

When we are agitated and troubled, especially when we are in disagreement with others who are partners or in our inner circle, what are we called to do? Why? What can we expect then in the process of going to unity?

Read Psalm 4:3–8:

3 But know that the LORD has set apart the godly for himself;
   the Lord hears when I call to him.
4 Be angry,[a] and do not sin;
   ponder in your own hearts on your beds, and be silent. *Selah*
5 Offer right sacrifices,
   and put your trust in the LORD.
6 There are many who say, "Who will show us some good?
   Lift up the light of your face upon us, O LORD!"
7 You have put more joy in my heart
   than they have when their grain and wine abound.
8 In peace I will both lie down and sleep;
   for you alone, O LORD, make me dwell in safety.

While we are processing disagreements, we can become agitated. He says, *Be angry and do not sin*. Is agitation sin? No, it is knowing something's not right, and we are not happy about this. It's OK to disagree or to say we are disappointed or this is something we are not happy with. He says we should first of all get our heart right—back to righteousness with Him.

The way to go to sin is to just keep plowing on with an attitude that we are going to take care of this, we are going to get our way, and we are going to battle. Before we crawl down that rabbit hole, know that it's OK to be frustrated and irritated, but we need to get our heart back to righteousness. By definition, if we do that, where have we gone? Into the Kingdom. He says, *Let Me give you some perspective here. Relax, go to forgiveness, and let Me help you understand what to do next. I'll give you the instruction, and the instruction will lead you to gladness. It'll go to the beautiful place of trust and confidence and resolution.* In doing this, we went from agitation to what? Joy and peace—because we stayed in that place of the Kingdom.

How do we resolve an issue when the other people involved don't want to participate in resolving it? What happens? They've got a problem. They don't want to deal with this at all. And they continue hurting us. They keep causing pain. They keep coming after us. God doesn't say He is going to provide resolution a certain way, and it might not be how we would want it resolved. Rather, it's God's truth. It could be that the truth is they're not changing. The truth is that they're going to keep coming after us. God says, *Let Me move or maneuver you this way and give you a solution—perhaps a border, something that I want you to do. Stop engaging. Don't worry, I'm going to take care of this because vengeance is Mine.* He'll give us an answer, so for us, it's resolved. The relationship isn't resolved, we are resolved. We're in alignment—beautiful alignment—with the truth of God that is righteousness, peace, and joy—the indicator that we now have resolution.

There's the indicator. We understand that vengeance is His, and justice will be served. It will be done. Remember the Covenant—He will bless those who bless us and curse those who curse us. We can move on and let go.

LESSON 4:
HOW DO WE LIVE IN THE KINGDOM ALL THE TIME?

As we cannot quite figure things out on our own, or are in disagreement with others regarding the solutions, what are we called to do? What then does God promise? Why is that important to us? What is the condition for us to receive this? Why?

Read James 1:2–8:

Testing of Your Faith

2 Count it all joy, my brothers,[a] when you meet trials of various kinds, 3 for you know that the testing of your faith produces steadfastness. 4 And let steadfastness have its full effect, that you may be perfect and complete, lacking in nothing.

5 If any of you lacks wisdom, let him ask God, who gives generously to all without reproach, and it will be given him. 6 But let him ask in faith, with no doubting, for the one who doubts is like a wave of the sea that is driven and tossed by the wind. 7 For that person must not suppose that he will receive anything from the Lord; 8 he is a double-minded man, unstable in all his ways.

____

____

____

____

____

When we are understanding God's will, He will ask us, *Do you believe it?* What then is He going to do? He is going to test us. The circumstances will go south. It's not happening as planned. Things aren't coming together. How will we respond? It doesn't matter, we believe it anyway. We are in peace, righteousness, and joy. Or, will we exit the Kingdom, complain about how awful things are and then go back to planning, worrying, fretting, and being anxious? If we fail the test, God simply says, *Come back, I have more work to do to move you to faith, believing what I have said*. The important thing about this test is for us to see that we don't have it so that we don't just skip it and move on without going to faith and receiving His answers and resolutions.

As we're in the middle of it, we are to ask for wisdom. He says He will give it to us, but to keep going. He doesn't mind. He is going to test us, and we are to cooperate with the test.

From the following two sets of verses—since we are called to live in the Kingdom, who is working to draw us out? What is his strategy for this? What is the outcome of this? How are we to avoid this and counteract this? Why is this so important?

Read James 1:12–18:

12 Blessed is the man who remains steadfast under trial, for when he has stood the test he will receive the crown of life, which God has promised to those who love him. 13 Let no one say when he is tempted, "I am being tempted by God," for God cannot be tempted with evil, and he himself tempts no one. 14 But each person is tempted when he is lured and enticed by his own desire. 15 Then desire when it has conceived gives birth to sin, and sin when it is fully grown brings forth death.

16 Do not be deceived, my beloved brothers. 17 Every good gift and every perfect gift is from above, coming down from the Father of lights, with whom there is no variation or shadow due to change.[a] 18 Of his own will he brought us forth by the word of truth, that we should be a kind of firstfruits of his creatures.

____

____

____

____

____

The enemy works by trying to cause us to go to sin. What would sin be? Not living in the Kingdom. It's that simple. The enemy works to get us out of the Kingdom, which is appealing to our self-determination, our flesh. That's sin nature. He appeals to our selfish desires. He says, _Well, what about this? Don't you think you should? Did God really say? Is that really going to happen? Why don't you? What about this?_ We're attracted to this and move with our own decisions to grasp it. The more that we're in the Kingdom, the more we will recognize when we have taken the bait of self and walked out the Kingdom. Fortunately, we have remedies.

LESSON 4:
HOW DO WE LIVE IN THE KINGDOM ALL THE TIME?

Read 1 Peter: 5:6–11:

6 Humble yourselves, therefore, under the mighty hand of God so that at the proper time he may exalt you, 7 casting all your anxieties on him, because he cares for you. 8 Be sober-minded; be watchful. Your adversary the devil prowls around like a roaring lion, seeking someone to devour. 9 Resist him, firm in your faith, knowing that the same kinds of suffering are being experienced by your brotherhood throughout the world. 10 And after you have suffered a little while, the God of all grace, who has called you to his eternal glory in Christ, will himself restore, confirm, strengthen, and establish you. 11 To him be the dominion forever and ever. Amen.

____

____

____

____

____

As we humble ourselves, come to God, and resist the devil, he has to flee. We say we don't need to put up with this, we see what happened here, but we are going to rebuke the devil so he's got to flee. Why? Because we went back to the Kingdom where he can't touch us. He can draw us out because we live in the world where things happen all the time. He can throw these grenades in front of us and cause us difficulty. Though we sometimes fall for it and exit the Kingdom, the remedy is to come on back, rebuke the devil, cast him out, stand against him and then do what? Humble ourselves by seeking God and His will again—in the Kingdom. *God, what do You have to say about this?* We just made a mess of it out there, but He says He understands that and can fix it. He might want to speak to us about why we keep walking out of the Kingdom. We've got a pattern, an issue. But if we let Him, He can heal those issues.

Having disagreements is normal. When we do, what is important as we move toward unity? How do we respond in the middle of the disagreement? Why is that so important to our life in the Kingdom?

Read Acts 15:1–3:

The Jerusalem Council
15 But some men came down from Judea and were teaching the brothers, "Unless you are circumcised according to the custom of Moses, you cannot be saved." [2] And after Paul and Barnabas had no small dissension and debate with them, Paul and Barnabas and some of the others were appointed to go up to Jerusalem to the apostles and the elders about this question. [3] So, being sent on their way by the church, they passed through both Phoenicia and Samaria, describing in detail the conversion of the Gentiles, and brought great joy to all the brothers.[a]

____

____

____

____

____

This is the issue of circumcision—it's the sign of the Covenant. Many were promoting that those who received the Covenant should physically be circumcised. Is this important? In a sense, yes. A messianic Jew understands salvation better than typical evangelicals who tend to think salvation is just a transaction—a ticket to heaven. The Messianic Jew sees it as a step into the Covenant—blessed to be a blessing. They also understood that the sign of the Covenant is circumcision. It wasn't such a bad thought, but they were adding it as a necessity to be saved, you also have to be circumcised physically. But Paul says that's not so. He said, *No, it's just Christ*. He did confirm the Covenant life but that the sign was Christ circumcising our heart—a spiritual thing. So, they had a big disagreement—a sharp disagreement that they could not get to resolution.

They all have the Holy Spirit, but in this disagreement situation, they just couldn't get there. So, they decided to go to Jerusalem and let the disciples help them. What did they do on the way? They had great joy and spread that joy even though they were in the middle of their disagreement. Yes. It was a huge disagreement, but they could still spread joy. Why? They were living in the Kingdom of God—the stuff of life. Are we going to have disagreements? Yes. Could somebody really be sharp against us? Yes. He said that it's OK, but to stay in peace. And while we're living our day out, live in joy and spread joy because it's a heart issue that demonstrates we are in the Kingdom of God.

From the following two sets of verses: What is important for us to enjoy the Kingdom? How do we practically do this? Why is this so important?

Read Philemon 1:4–7:

Philemon's Love and Faith

4 I thank my God always when I remember you in my prayers, 5 because I hear of your love and of the faith that you have toward the Lord Jesus and for all the saints, 6 and I pray that the sharing of your faith may become effective for the full knowledge of every good thing that is in us for the sake of Christ.[a] 7 For I have derived much joy and comfort from your love, my brother, because the hearts of the saints have been refreshed through you.

____

____

____

____

____

Joy. The hearts of the saints have been refreshed as we're in fellowship with each other. Think about how critical this is. Here's the question: Are we in sweet fellowship with other believers who know how to live in the Kingdom and keep us and all the group in joy? Or are we in a place where there is contention, jealousy, manipulation, where games are being played, and we are not pleasant or in the sweetness? God says, *The body of Christ is supposed to be joyful*. Why? We all are to live in the Kingdom and help each other stay in the Kingdom, even when we have disagreement, which is normal and OK. Life together in the Kingdom is full of fun and joy and excitement to be together. We can't wait to get together. There's a sweetness, there's an excitement, there's a sharing, there's celebration.

Read Deuteronomy 16:13–17:

The Feast of Booths

[13] "You shall keep the Feast of Booths seven days, when you have gathered in the produce from your threshing floor and your winepress. [14] You shall rejoice in your feast, you and your son and your daughter, your male servant and your female servant, the Levite, the sojourner, the fatherless, and the widow who are within your towns. [15] For seven days you shall keep the feast to the LORD your God at the place that the LORD will choose, because the LORD your God will bless you in all your produce and in all the work of your hands, so that you will be altogether joyful.

[16] "Three times a year all your males shall appear before the LORD your God at the place that he will choose: at the Feast of Unleavened Bread, at the Feast of Weeks, and at the Feast of Booths. They shall not appear before the LORD empty-handed. [17] Every man shall give as he is able, according to the blessing of the Lord your God that he has given you.

____

____

____

____

____

He says that the things that He performs for us, the beautiful resolution of life are to be celebrated. Have fun, rejoice, dance, sing, relax. Get good at that. Take the time to get together with family and small groups, and have feasting and joy.

As we complete this lesson, we've learned this aspect of pursuing truth, seeking God's will, and letting Him answer us. He said for us to go to unity. He will confirm that with us and will use others to do it. Stay in fellowship with others, be in the body, stimulate each other. Refresh each other. Spread joy, the joy that's happening to us. As God works with us, let Him wall up the patterns that the enemy keeps bringing out. Rejoice because we can stay in that beautiful place.

LESSON 5:
WHAT ARE THE PRACTICAL WAYS OF ENJOYING THE KINGDOM AND OUR ASSIGNMENT OF GIVING IT AWAY TO OTHERS?

As we conclude our course: *Living in the Kingdom of God—Righteousness, Peace, and Joy,* and are now living in that Kingdom, this final section will cover how we are called to give it away. The reason that we're living in this Kingdom is because Christ is righteousness, peace, and joy. That is what the Kingdom is all about, and we, in a simple way, are walking with Him. We're in Him. We've surrendered our will to Him. We're letting Him be the King in this Kingdom and not us. That's where all this deliverance comes from. Resolution of issues, the opportunity to restore things, the transformation of our lives, the joy of the things that He has for us is all there. He said our role is to understand His mission, which is to deliver the Covenant. He is going to bless us to make us a blessing. He's calling us to join Him in the abundant, rather, the super-abundant life that He's giving to us, and He's going to fulfill His good plan for us in the Kingdom of God. We learned that our role is to seek His will, to ask Him what He has to say about all of our issues, to believe that He has truth and guidance and wisdom to get us through it, to celebrate with other believers, to be in fellowship with other believers, and to keep remembering the Covenant, which is what He's going to deliver.

And as we do, we will experience the fullness of the Kingdom, and we will have joy—not a fake joy or joy that only comes once in a while, but rather real joy because it's coming from Him. As we experience this, we are then called to give it away, and invite others to the same place.

From the following five sets of verses, how does God describe the elements of the Kingdom that are to bring us joy and excitement? How do we experience these practically in our lives? Why are these so important to our life in the Kingdom?

> **"He's calling us to join Him in the abundant, rather, the super-abundant life that He's giving to us, and He's going to fulfill His good plan for us in the Kingdom of God."**

Read Ecclesiastes 2:24–26:

24 There is nothing better for a person than that he should eat and drink and find enjoyment[a] in his toil. This also, I saw, is from the hand of God, 25 for apart from him[b] who can eat

> or who can have enjoyment? [26] For to the one who pleases him God has given wisdom and knowledge and joy, but to the sinner he has given the business of gathering and collecting, only to give to one who pleases God. This also is vanity and a striving after wind.

____

____

____

____

He says He wants us to find joy, a rejoicing celebration in our work. This is from God. So, one of our highest callings is to find joy in our work. That's an indicator of us being in the Kingdom. Does that mean that there's never any difficulty or trouble in that work? No. He's saying that we are fundamentally in sync with who He made us to be, that we're enjoying the environment, we're enjoying the culture, we're enjoying the work that we're involved in. But through the trouble, we know that He is going to bring resolution to the issues of our life, and we're leaving the outcome to Him. It's a fundamental question: either we are or we are not. If the answer is no, not really, what would we say then? We need to go ask God to direct us so that we can enjoy our work again. We are not to presume the answer. It could be that we are in the right place, but that we've got a heart issue, and our joy is being stolen, not by the work, but by something else. Let Him help us with that. Maybe we are angry at somebody at work? He can resolve that as we go to forgiveness and receive His instruction for reconciliation. Perhaps we're in the wrong spot. What we're doing doesn't match up with how He has made us to be. Maybe He has a new place for us.

> **Read Ecclesiastes 3:9–12:**
>
> The God-Given Task
> 9 What gain has the worker from his toil? 10 I have seen the business that God has given to the children of man to be busy with. 11 He has made everything beautiful in its time. Also, he has put eternity into man's heart, yet so that he cannot find out what God has done from the beginning to the end. 12 I perceived that there is nothing better for them than to be joyful and to do good as long as they live.

____

____

____

____

____

God's questions to us are: *Are you experiencing joy and gladness in the things of life – your spouse, your work? Are you enjoying what I'm giving you?* And again, it's a simple response: either *yes* or *no*. If no, we are not to go change it on our own but ask the Father. *God, something is not right here. Please guide us and lead us into what Your answer would be for us to have joy.* And then follow Him into His place.

> **Read Ecclesiastes 5:18–20:**
>
> 18 Behold, what I have seen to be good and fitting is to eat and drink and find enjoyment[a] in all the toil with which one toils under the sun the few days of his life that God has given him, for this is his lot. 19 Everyone also to whom God has given wealth and possessions and power to enjoy them, and to accept his lot and rejoice in his toil—this is the gift of God. 20 For he will not much remember the days of his life because God keeps him occupied with joy in his heart.

____

____

____

____

____

He uses the word *enjoy*—enjoy where we are—rejoicing with gladness of heart, celebrating, mirth, gaiety. Are we experiencing that or not? Are we experiencing God's highest and best for us?

Read Ecclesiastes 8:15:

15 And I commend joy, for man has nothing better under the sun but to eat and drink and be joyful, for this will go with him in his toil through the days of his life that God has given him under the sun.

____

____

____

____

____

There's nothing better than eating, drinking, and being merry—in all of life. It looks like fellowship around the table. We're with other people, we're enjoying what we're doing—not too busy, not to occupied to enjoy all this, but rather, we are in concert with other people who also live in joy with us—having merriment together.

Read Ecclesiastes 9:7–10:

Enjoy Life with the One You Love

[7] Go, eat your bread with joy, and drink your wine with a merry heart, for God has already approved what you do.

[8] Let your garments be always white. Let not oil be lacking on your head.

[9] Enjoy life with the wife whom you love, all the days of your vain[a] life that he has given you under the sun, because that is your portion in life and in your toil at which you toil under the sun. [10] Whatever your hand finds to do, do it with your might,[b] for there is no work or thought or knowledge or wisdom in Sheol, to which you are going.

____

____

____

____

____

He says, *Enjoy your spouse—getting sweetness because you love being together, and you're thrilled to be together—getting sweeter, sweeter, and sweeter.* All who are in fellowship together (especially spouses) are living in the Kingdom of God, having adventure together, experiencing stimulating life together.

What did the disciples experience when Jesus appeared in the upper room with them after the resurrection? Why was that so important to them? What did Jesus say regarding how He was sending them? What does that look like practically for us? Why is this so important to life in the Kingdom?

Read John 20:19–23:

Jesus Appears to the Disciples

[19] On the evening of that day, the first day of the week, the doors being locked where the disciples were for fear of the Jews,[a] Jesus came and stood among them and said to them, "Peace be with you." [20] When he had said this, he showed

> them his hands and his side. Then the disciples were glad when they saw the Lord. [21] Jesus said to them again, "Peace be with you. As the Father has sent me, even so I am sending you." [22] And when he had said this, he breathed on them and said to them, "Receive the Holy Spirit. [23] If you forgive the sins of any, they are forgiven them; if you withhold forgiveness from any, it is withheld."

____

____

____

____

When the disciples were so discouraged, believing that their life with Christ was over, and they had wasted three years of their life, Christ appears through the door and speaks, *Peace/Shalom*. They were glad, joyful. Hallelujah, we get to be with Him still. And then He says, *As the Father has sent Me, I'm sending you.* OK. How did the Father send Him? By following what the Father spoke, instructed, and saw wherever He was. In the same way that He has been sent by living in the Kingdom and receiving His instruction from God, He is sending us. We are to always get our instructions from God, the Father. We are to live that way. He is going to give us instruction. He is going to give us assignments. He is going to say what He would like us to do now. Who is giving us our assignments? It's not us, not our friends, not our church—it's God.

We have the privilege of joining God in His work—by following the assignment given by God—not assignments given by a program, but His direction, and often these assignments revolve around relationships that need strengthening—such as with a spouse, children, employees, etc.

From the following two sets of verses—describe all the elements and steps that God provided for Esther to be in the position to serve God's purposes. What was her initial response to the assignment? Why? What then did she understand, and why is this so important to fulfilling God's assignment? What then is unique about our assignments? Why is that important for us?

Read Esther 4:1–14:

Esther Agrees to Help the Jews

4 When Mordecai learned all that had been done, Mordecai tore his clothes and put on sackcloth and ashes, and went out into the midst of the city, and he cried out with a loud and bitter cry. ² He went up to the entrance of the king's gate, for no one was allowed to enter the king's gate clothed in sackcloth. ³ And in every province, wherever the king's command and his decree reached, there was great mourning among the Jews, with fasting and weeping and lamenting, and many of them lay in sackcloth and ashes.

⁴ When Esther's young women and her eunuchs came and told her, the queen was deeply distressed. She sent garments to clothe Mordecai, so that he might take off his sackcloth, but he would not accept them. ⁵ Then Esther called for Hathach, one of the king's eunuchs, who had been appointed to attend her, and ordered him to go to Mordecai to learn what this was and why it was. ⁶ Hathach went out to Mordecai in the open square of the city in front of the king's gate, ⁷ and Mordecai told him all that had happened to him, and the exact sum of money that Haman had promised to pay into the king's treasuries for the destruction of the Jews. ⁸ Mordecai also gave him a copy of the written decree issued in Susa for their destruction,[a] that he might show it to Esther and explain it to her and command her to go to the king to beg his favor and plead with him[b] on behalf of her people. ⁹ And Hathach went and told Esther what Mordecai had said. ¹⁰ Then Esther spoke to Hathach and commanded him to go to Mordecai and say, ¹¹ "All the king's servants and the people of the king's provinces know that if any man or woman goes to the king inside the inner court without being called, there is but one law—to be put to death, except the one to whom the king holds out the golden scepter so that he may live. But as for me, I have not been called to come in to the king these thirty days."

> [12] And they told Mordecai what Esther had said. [13] Then Mordecai told them to reply to Esther, "Do not think to yourself that in the king's palace you will escape any more than all the other Jews. [14] For if you keep silent at this time, relief and deliverance will rise for the Jews from another place, but you and your father's house will perish. And who knows whether you have not come to the kingdom for such a time as this?"

____

____

____

____

____

What was the problem here? There was a decree sent to destroy all Jews. They were going to be killed through the manipulation of Haman. Mordechai is mourning and saying, *This can't be of God—I repent, and I'm sorry*. Esther is the queen now, and Esther is what? A Jew. She's been raised up to queen through a sequence of God placing her in the court of the king who fell in love with her and gave her favor. God's work put her as the queen next to the king. Since she is in this position, Mordechai tells her to go talk to the king and tell him to stop it. How does Esther respond? *I can't*. This what's called a *sticky wicket*—a double bind. *The king may or may not agree to that, but if I go to appeal, he's going to kill me before I even get to appeal.* So as far as she's concerned, the answer to the dilemma is what? There isn't any solution. She is stuck. She has a problem.

Read Esther 8:7–17:

> [7] Then King Ahasuerus said to Queen Esther and to Mordecai the Jew, "Behold, I have given Esther the house of Haman, and they have hanged him on the gallows,[a] because he intended to lay hands on the Jews. [8] But you may write as you please with regard to the Jews, in the name of the king, and seal it with the king's ring, for an edict written in the name of the king and sealed with the king's ring cannot be revoked."

[9] The king's scribes were summoned at that time, in the third month, which is the month of Sivan, on the twenty-third day. And an edict was written, according to all that Mordecai commanded concerning the Jews, to the satraps and the governors and the officials of the provinces from India to Ethiopia, 127 provinces, to each province in its own script and to each people in its own language, and also to the Jews in their script and their language. [10] And he wrote in the name of King Ahasuerus and sealed it with the king's signet ring. Then he sent the letters by mounted couriers riding on swift horses that were used in the king's service, bred from the royal stud, [11] saying that the king allowed the Jews who were in every city to gather and defend their lives, to destroy, to kill, and to annihilate any armed force of any people or province that might attack them, children and women included, and to plunder their goods, [12] on one day throughout all the provinces of King Ahasuerus, on the thirteenth day of the twelfth month, which is the month of Adar. [13] A copy of what was written was to be issued as a decree in every province, being publicly displayed to all peoples, and the Jews were to be ready on that day to take vengeance on their enemies. [14] So the couriers, mounted on their swift horses that were used in the king's service, rode out hurriedly, urged by the king's command. And the decree was issued in Susa the citadel.

[15] Then Mordecai went out from the presence of the king in royal robes of blue and white, with a great golden crown[b] and a robe of fine linen and purple, and the city of Susa shouted and rejoiced. [16] The Jews had light and gladness and joy and honor. [17] And in every province and in every city, wherever the king's command and his edict reached, there was gladness and joy among the Jews, a feast and a holiday. And many from the peoples of the country declared themselves Jews, for fear of the Jews had fallen on them.

Esther said, *No, I'm not going to do it.*

Mordechai said, *Well, I don't think you're following God's will. I would like you to reconsider and go to God.*

She goes to God, and God says: *Yes, I want you to do this.*

And then Mordecai says, *I believe that you've been set up for such a time as this. You have been put by God in this position so that you can do and fulfill what His call is to you.*

Esther prayed about that and said, *I'm willing—if I die, I die. If that's the outcome, so be it, because I'm going to follow the assignment from God (even if it is negative for me). I'm going to fulfill that assignment,* which she did.

When the king asked her what is going on, she related that Haman was manipulating him and working to kill her people, and Mordecai even got him to sign a decree for that. The king said that was absurd and reversed it. Haman had erected gallows to hang Mordechai, but the king said that since he had done this dastardly thing, to go ahead and hang him on the gallows that he had prepared. (Covenant of God—curse those who curse us). Then he said he was going to make a decree that would not only protect her people but would go after her enemies. The Jews went from fear to what? Great security, safety, and protection under the king who was unknowingly going to kill them. Their response was great joy, great gladness, great celebration because they were following the will of God. Esther had received that assignment, and it had big implications because of God's bigger story of His Kingdom.

We are going to have assignments all the time. He'd like us to speak to certain people. He'd like us to assist somebody who is struggling. Maybe it's a fellow believer who is sad, in mourning, experiencing difficulties, having trouble. He is giving us that assignment. Why is He giving that assignment to us? So we can do what He says. Whatever the case or assignment might be, we should appreciate the significance of the fact that He chose us to fulfill it. He selected us to bring His message and gave us the opportunity to bring them joy, gladness, and life.

God says: *I've selected you because you're the only one. If you don't, there's nobody else to do it.* This is very significant as this assignment is for "such a time as this." It happens all the time.

LESSON 5:
WHAT ARE THE PRACTICAL WAYS OF ENJOYING THE KINGDOM AND OUR ASSIGNMENT OF GIVING IT AWAY TO OTHERS?

What ultimately is the purpose of us living in the Kingdom? Why? On what basis can we fulfill this? Why?

Read Isaiah 40:5–9:

5 And the glory of the Lord shall be revealed,
    and all flesh shall see it together,
    for the mouth of the Lord has spoken."

The Word of God Stands Forever
6 A voice says, "Cry!"
    And I said,[a] "What shall I cry?"
All flesh is grass,
    and all its beauty[b] is like the flower of the field.
7 The grass withers, the flower fades
    when the breath of the Lord blows on it;
    surely the people are grass.
8 The grass withers, the flower fades,
    but the word of our God will stand forever.

The Greatness of God
9 Go on up to a high mountain,
    O Zion, herald of good news;[c]
lift up your voice with strength,
    O Jerusalem, herald of good news;[d]
    lift it up, fear not;
say to the cities of Judah,
    "Behold your God!"

____
____
____
____

God does not give His glory to anybody else. This is all for His glory. Now, the reason that we can experience His glory is because we're living where? In the Kingdom, following the King—where He is doing supernatural work, which we then automatically glorify Him. He is not giving His glory to another because anybody outside the Kingdom doesn't have the opportunity to experience His glory. They can never give it to Him anyway. He is not going to share it with anybody, but we are going to experience it.

He then gives us a deeper understanding of this. He is sending us as what? The Covenant. We are the Covenant. So, His assignment is actually to be a purveyor of the Covenant. It's us. But it's actually not us. Who is it? Christ in us—the hope of glory. Those who aren't living in the Kingdom can see the light of that, and we're inviting them to Christ because they see us living a different life. Where? In the Kingdom—the life of the Kingdom is being experienced. And because of that, we become the Covenant. We bring the Covenant and others see what our life looks like, and then they have a desire to be part of that. *Can I experience this too? Yes, let me walk with you to have you learn to live in and experience the Kingdom of God—the Covenant life.*

Since we are called to give it away, how is that to work? What does this mean regarding our approach to this? How do we vary our steps based upon how others respond? Why is that important, and what does that mean for how we live in the Kingdom?

Read Luke 10:1–13:

Jesus Sends Out the Seventy-Two
10 After this the Lord appointed seventy-two[a] others and sent them on ahead of him, two by two, into every town and place where he himself was about to go. [2] And he said to them, "The harvest is plentiful, but the laborers are few. Therefore pray earnestly to the Lord of the harvest to send out laborers into his harvest. [3] Go your way; behold, I am sending you out as lambs in the midst of wolves. [4] Carry no moneybag, no knapsack, no sandals, and greet no one on the road. [5] Whatever house you enter, first say, 'Peace be to this house!' [6] And if a son of peace is there, your peace will rest upon him. But if not, it will return to you. [7] And remain in the same house, eating and drinking what they provide, for the laborer deserves his wages. Do not go from house to house. [8] Whenever you enter a town and they receive you, eat what is set before you. [9] Heal the

> sick in it and say to them, 'The kingdom of God has come near to you.' [10] But whenever you enter a town and they do not receive you, go into its streets and say, [11] 'Even the dust of your town that clings to our feet we wipe off against you. Nevertheless know this, that the kingdom of God has come near.' [12] I tell you, it will be more bearable on that day for Sodom than for that town.
>
> Woe to Unrepentant Cities
> [13] "Woe to you, Chorazin! Woe to you, Bethsaida! For if the mighty works done in you had been done in Tyre and Sidon, they would have repented long ago, sitting in sackcloth and ashes.

____

____

____

____

____

Notice a statement here, *Say to them, "The Kingdom of God has come near to you."* The Kingdom of God is here, and we're offering our shalom so that others may experience this Kingdom. He is offering us the opportunity to experience—to tell them the Kingdom is here. This is interesting. Why is the Kingdom here? Because we're here. It's us. We're walking in the Kingdom. The Kingdom goes with us because its spiritual, and it is in and with us since we are surrendered to the King, living in the Kingdom. We are to tell them that and offer our peace, our shalom. If they receive it (what we're offering to them), they too will learn to live in the Kingdom, experience the Kingdom life, and will also be given the assignment of being the Covenant and giving it away to others—multiplication, which is God's way of inviting others to the Kingdom.

We appeal to the difficult circumstances that they are experiencing since they are not living in the Kingdom. *I can guarantee you that God will restore your life, resolve your difficult issue, and give you a grand life, the super-abundant life, in the Kingdom. Do you have a heart to go to the Kingdom?* They have to say, *Yes, I'm willing to go*—especially since they do not know much about it and are likely to begin to have doubt. All they can relate to is observing us and our life in the Kingdom. If they say, *Yes, I would like to, that is wonderful*—stay with them. Don't go from thing to thing to thing or leave them without learning the Kingdom. Stay with them and help them understand the Kingdom.

There will be some who say, *No, I don't want to. I'm not interested in that.* Others might say *yes*, but actually mean *no*. Here's what happens, people say, *Yeah, I'd like to do that* and are then given scripture to go process to learn the life of the Kingdom. When they are finished with it and have processed it (by writing out the scripture and what it says to them), we plan to get together and process what this means for them learning to live in the Kingdom. But even after a few attempts to encourage them to process the truth this way (learning to abide and hear God's voice personally) some never follow through or they have lost their interest in the Kingdom and have fallen back into their woe. They never get to the scripture and don't understand that it's the Kingdom of God that's going to make the difference. When they say no or don't follow through by getting into the Word, what are we to do then?

Move on. Take our peace back. Dust off our feet (leave nothing of their refusal to stay on us) and tell them that the Kingdom was here but they rejected it. But if, at a later time, they come back and say they'd like to re-engage and learn the Kingdom life—what would our response be? Absolutely. Come on. Why can we easily do this? Because we're not taking the responsibility of the outcome. Even if they end up living in the Kingdom, it's not our choice, and it's not our burden. We're being sent by God to offer it. He will tell us who and when, and as we do, be faithful to that. Don't worry about the outcome. Don't be responsible for whether they do or don't. Just be faithful by offering our peace. Since this is our assignment, what's is important for us? We have to be in the Kingdom. We have to have and be experiencing peace, which is then ours to offer. It's not telling a story about God—it's the life of God.

What is important for us to understand as we fulfill God's assignments for us? What does He care about and why? Why is this important to us?

Read Matthew 25:14–30:

The Parable of the Talents
14 "For it will be like a man going on a journey, who called his servants[a] and entrusted to them his property. 15 To one he gave five talents,[b] to another two, to another one, to each according to his ability. Then he went away. 16 He who had received the five talents went at once and traded with them, and he made five talents more. 17 So also he who had the two talents made two talents more. 18 But he who had received the one talent went and dug in the

ground and hid his master's money. [19] Now after a long time the master of those servants came and settled accounts with them. [20] And he who had received the five talents came forward, bringing five talents more, saying, 'Master, you delivered to me five talents; here, I have made five talents more.' [21] His master said to him, 'Well done, good and faithful servant.[c] You have been faithful over a little; I will set you over much. Enter into the joy of your master.' [22] And he also who had the two talents came forward, saying, 'Master, you delivered to me two talents; here, I have made two talents more.' [23] His master said to him, 'Well done, good and faithful servant. You have been faithful over a little; I will set you over much. Enter into the joy of your master.' [24] He also who had received the one talent came forward, saying, 'Master, I knew you to be a hard man, reaping where you did not sow, and gathering where you scattered no seed, [25] so I was afraid, and I went and hid your talent in the ground. Here, you have what is yours.' [26] But his master answered him, 'You wicked and slothful servant! You knew that I reap where I have not sown and gather where I scattered no seed? [27] Then you ought to have invested my money with the bankers, and at my coming I should have received what was my own with interest. [28] So take the talent from him and give it to him who has the ten talents. [29] For to everyone who has will more be given, and he will have an abundance. But from the one who has not, even what he has will be taken away. [30] And cast the worthless servant into the outer darkness. In that place there will be weeping and gnashing of teeth.'

Look at the one who had five talents, who had a larger return than the one who had two talents. What did he say to both of them? *Well done, good and faithful servant.* What's being faithful to the master? Using what He's giving us and being obedient to the assignment given to us by the Master. He further states that because the servant had been faithful over a few things, over small things, He will give them more.

There's the test of it—not deciding on our own to try to do big stuff for the Master, for God. Rather, are we faithful to the small stuff? What is His assignment for us? He said there's no difference in how He ranks these assignments or compares the assignments. The key is to do the assignment that He gives us in a way that we, too, will be told, *Well done, good and faithful servant.*

The reward is to receive more—and really is about receiving more authority, more power in the assignments that He give us—more, but not necessarily bigger in natural scope (more people, bigger program, etc.). He is going to keep having us experience His authority as we live it out and enter into what? His joy. Why? Because we're experiencing the thrill of following His assignments and we're faithful.

The master in this case was looking at the result but deeper than that—he was looking at the heart. Did the servant have a heart to be faithful to what he asked him to do? That's why the reward is the same—because he's not focusing on the result. Rather, do we have a heart to follow Him and His assignment? If so, we are faithful in our heart, and we get the reward. What is the reward? Joy. There's joy in the assignment, there's joy in the process, and there is joy in an assignment well done. The well done isn't the outcome, it's the heart. Do we have a heart to go? As we do that, teach and disciple others.

LESSON 5:
WHAT ARE THE PRACTICAL WAYS OF ENJOYING THE KINGDOM AND OUR ASSIGNMENT OF GIVING IT AWAY TO OTHERS?

From the following two sets of verses—as we live out the life of the Kingdom and give it away, what does God want us to enjoy, receive, and experience? How and why?

> **Read 3 John 1:1–4:**
>
> Greeting
> [1] The elder to the beloved Gaius, whom I love in truth.
>
> [2] Beloved, I pray that all may go well with you and that you may be in good health, as it goes well with your soul. [3] For I rejoiced greatly when the brothers[a] came and testified to your truth, as indeed you are walking in the truth. [4] I have no greater joy than to hear that my children are walking in the truth.

____

____

____

____

____

There's no greater joy than His children (followers who learned this and their followers who learned) so it's children and grandchildren, offspring, who are walking in the truth. But as spiritual offspring, it's not our physical children (although it can be), but it's the people who we've given it away to and discipled, shared, and helped them understand that this is the way to live life. There's no greater joy than what? Him seeing us living in the Kingdom. There's nothing better than to see our offspring walking in the truth, walking in the Kingdom. It is our heart to live in the Kingdom, then give it away so that others live in the Kingdom, who then give it away as well. There is nothing better.

Read Jude 1:24–25:

Doxology

24 Now to him who is able to keep you from stumbling and to present you blameless before the presence of his glory with great joy, 25 to the only God, our Savior, through Jesus Christ our Lord, be glory, majesty, dominion, and authority, before all time[a] and now and forever. Amen.

____

____

____

____

____

We are to pray and receive—*May Jesus Christ and the Kingdom of God, be operational for you forever and ever*—our prayer all the time.

Read Numbers 6:22–27:

Aaron's Blessing

22 The LORD spoke to Moses, saying, 23 "Speak to Aaron and his sons, saying, Thus you shall bless the people of Israel: you shall say to them,

24 The LORD bless you and keep you;

25 the LORD make his face to shine upon you and be gracious to you;

26 the LORD lift up his countenance[a] upon you and give you peace.

27 "So shall they put my name upon the people of Israel, and I will bless them."

____

____

____

____

____

LESSON 5:
WHAT ARE THE PRACTICAL WAYS OF ENJOYING THE KINGDOM AND OUR ASSIGNMENT OF GIVING IT AWAY TO OTHERS?

As we finish this course, our life is to be experiencing the Kingdom of God. May we see and experience God face to face. And may He give us His shalom. He is shalom—His righteousness, peace, and joy in the Holy Spirit. Join Him there. May that be characteristic of our life where we live it out all the time. It doesn't matter what our circumstances are; it doesn't matter that there are difficult things, including conflict issues. Are we going to have those things? Yes. But in the Kingdom, because it is righteousness, peace, and joy in the Holy Spirit, we will remain in the peace and joy of the Kingdom. This is the indicator that we are living in the Kingdom because He is righteousness, peace, and joy, and He'll give it to us right now. He's going to resolve the issues of life—which we are going to have—and He will give us hope and excitement and joy.

living waters
Abide™
MINISTRIES

History of
Abide Ministries

In the 1990s, Rich and Linda Case received a call from God to dig into what it means to truly live in the Spirit.

In the 1990s, Rich and Linda Case received a call from God to dig into what it means to truly live in the Spirit. They had been believers for most of their lives and regularly attended church and Bible studies, but began to realize that, despite knowing the Bible intellectually, their personal experiences seemed disconnected from the promises and truths found in scripture. As they then learned these essential truths through their abiding and hearing God's voice — and began to see the grand life play out in their lives God called them to give that knowledge away. In 2001, God initiated the ABIDE ministry at a retreat with friends in Austria, and through their personal experience of this abiding life, their friends noticed the change in their lives and inquired if Rich and Linda could host a similar retreat the following year. This was repeated three years in a row, and then God called them to host weekend retreats in their home in Colorado.

Through the formal development of the truths revealed by God with Abiding and additional electives, they founded All for Jesus — Living Waters Ministries, now Abide Ministries — and have seen it grow exponentially since then, with 24+ retreat leaders all over the world, 29 online courses, eight books on various aspects of living life with Christ, and a daily podcast. Rich and Linda have also worked with various churches to strengthening them with the truths of an abiding life in Christ, and seeing Christ bring reconciliation and new vision to desperate situations.

Their heart is to bring the truths and promises of God to as many people as possible, showing everyone that when you abide in Christ and seek Him daily, your life can be completely and utterly transformed — enabling you to experience the grand life promised by God.

Vision

At our core, we believe in walking along God's path and connecting to the vine (abiding). As we walk in unity with others and understand God's Word as the truth, we are sure to experience His promised grand life and thus, willingly accept God's will as our chosen path.

Mission

1. Live out and invite everyone to experience the grand, spectacular, abundant life by hearing God's voice.
2. Share God's majesty, a close relationship with us as he yearns for our restoration.
3. God is majestic, grand and pure goodness, so that we can experience His nature in real life.
4. Communicate to everyone, irrespective of their condition, that all are meant to experience God's Divine Life (grand, majestic), by receiving His personal plan for us.
5. God delivers this life for us in a SUPERNATURAL way, transcending human comprehension, and thus, becoming normal in our life.
6. Teach that personal truths are revealed to us by God, grounded on His word – the embodiment of Truth.
7. Recognize that abiding in Christ changes our life in tangible, real ways, and is not just learning about or studying this life.
8. Teach that as we abide in Christ, we learn to understand and amp; follow God's will for our lives, as He leads us personally into His grand, Divine plan for us. His personal plan calls us into His bigger story with our best interest at heart (blessed to bless others).

Statement of Non-Profit Status

Abide Ministries is a not-for-profit 501(c)3 organization that has been fully funded by our founders, leaders and retreat participants since its inception.

Tax-ID number: 27-1731819

Testimonies

"If I'm not abiding, I feel like I'm dying. Abiding is living...It's powerful to know that you have God's perspective on something."

 Steve

"This was the first time that I understood what people meant by God's living Word. And I've been a Christian for a lot of years, but this was the first time it really came alive for me and I really could experience that."

 Dan

"It doesn't matter where you are at in your walk. If you just got saved yesterday or if you've been a 20+ year believer like i have, learning how to hear God's voice and learning His will is just as important in day one as it is in day 3,426. You wanna hear God's will and this course has helped me hear Him more clearly."

 Bob

"Abiding turned out to be the most transformational thing I've ever had since salvation in my Christian walk and in our marriage, and it's just been amazing. God has a path for us and He is there and He's showing it to us."

 Heath

"Before, in my quiet time, it was more of a checklist thing for me to do in the morning, and, honestly, some mornings it was the thing that went if I was busy, and some days it didn't even happen. Now, it's become so personal to me and the time flies by in the morning and God speaks so directly to me and I just never felt that way on a daily basis before. That has been life-altering for me."

 Rebecca

"I heard about people living in peace, I heard about people living in joy, and realizing all kinds of things around them are happening. And then we realize, wait a minute, we're there, we have peace beyond understanding."

 Brad

Giving to the Ministry

Have you experienced abundant blessing from your time with Abide Ministries?

Pay it forward by donating at **abideministries.com/donate** and help us support others in learning how to seek Christ and abide in Him! We appreciate your desire to help us share the Abundant Life with the rest of the world.

Learn More at
abideministries.com

Podcast

Escape the chaos and uncertainty of the world with our podcast, *"Come and See, Finding Truth in a World of Chaos,"* available on YouTube, Apple Podcasts, and Spotify.

CHANNEL

PLAYLIST PAGE

Tune in five days a week as our hosts, Rich Case and Kathy Rocconi, dive into the scriptures and discuss what it looks like to live an abiding life with Christ. Join us as we seek God's truth in a world of turmoil and darkness.

Online
Courses

Abide Ministries online courses uncover life-changing biblical truths, with practical application and wisdom. Our courses are joyful and life-giving and are perfect for small groups as well as individuals.

Each course has an accompanying workbook. Join us as we learn about biblical topics like Hearing God's Voice, Discerning God's Will, the Covenant, Living in Forgiveness, Living in the Kingdom of God, Living in the Supernatural, Christ, Clutter and the Calendar, Living the Grand Life, and many, many more.

COURSES

Do you have friends or a small group that you would like to experience what you just experienced?

Would you be interested in attending another retreat, which we call electives to go deeper in your walk with God?

See the various options on our website.
The topics for retreats and courses are the same.